Errata Sheet for California Politics and Government: A Practical Approach
Larry N. Gerston and Terry Christensen

ISBN-10: 0495913456

We completed the eleventh edition of *California Politics and Government: A Practical Approach* on November 5, 2010, three days after the fall elections and in time for use during the Spring 2011 semester. This has been our custom with each edition. At that time, the attorney general's race was extremely tight. Republican Steve Cooley was leading Democrat Kamala Harris by 34,000 votes of the more than 7,000,000 counted; the remaining two million votes would not be counted for several weeks. Ultimately, Harris overcame the deficit and won by about 50,000 votes in one of the tightest statewide contests on record. Why did Harris ultimately prevail? One reason is because of the 13 point registration edge Democrats enjoyed over Republicans, affirming that "political party" still means something in California. Another reason is that Cooley, the popular district attorney in Los Angeles County, did not even carry his own county. Clearly, "retail politics," the idea of candidates mixing it up with the people worked much better for Harris than her opponent. The bottom line: Kamala Harris emerged as the victor. Please bear this in mind when you read about the attorney general on page 104.

The election of Kamala Harris brings up another correction: we note on page 34 that Deborah Bowen currently is the only female holding statewide office. Of course, Harris' election adds a second female to the list. Moreover, she is the only female of color to hold statewide office.

✳

California Politics
and Government

California Politics and Government

A Practical Approach

ELEVENTH EDITION

LARRY N. GERSTON
San Jose State University

TERRY CHRISTENSEN
San Jose State University

WADSWORTH
CENGAGE Learning™

Australia • Brazil • Japan • Korea • Mexico • Singapore • Spain • United Kingdom • United States

WADSWORTH
CENGAGE Learning™

California Politics and Government: A Practical Approach, Eleventh Edition
Larry N. Gerston, Terry Christensen

Senior Publisher: Suzanne Jeans

Executive Editor: Carolyn Merrill

Marketing Manager: Lydia Lestar

Editorial Assistant: Nina Wasserman

Media Editor: Laura Hildebrand

Marketing Coordinator: Josh Hendrick

Marketing Communications Manager: Heather Baxley

Content Project Manager: Susan Miscio

Senior Art Director: Linda Helcher

Production Technology Analyst: Jeff Joubert

Print Buyer: Fola Orekoya

Senior Rights Acquisition Manager, Text: Katie Huha

Production Service: Macmillan Publishing Services

Cover Designer: Lou Ann Thesing

Cover Image: Golden gate bridge ©Cheng Chang/istockphoto
Beach ©Lee Pettet/istockphoto
Wind Turbine ©EuToch/istockphoto
Flag ©Lee Pettet/istockphoto
Buildings ©S. Greg Panosian/istockphoto
Surfers ©DNY59/istockphoto
Vineyard ©Galina Barskaya/istockphoto
Jerry Brown © Justin Sullivan/©Getty Images

Compositor: MPS Limited, a Macmillan Company

For product information and technology assistance, contact us at **Cengage Learning Customer & Sales Support, 1-800-354-9706**

For permission to use material from this text or product, submit all requests online at **www.cengage.com/permissions**.
Further permissions questions can be e-mailed to **permissionrequest@cengage.com**

Library of Congress Control Number: 2010939141

ISBN-13: 978-0-495-91345-0
ISBN-10: 0-495-91345-6

Wadsworth
20 Channel Center Street
Boston, MA 02210
USA

Cengage Learning is a leading provider of customized learning solutions with office locations around the globe, including Singapore, the United Kingdom, Australia, Mexico, Brazil and Japan. Locate your local office at **international.cengage.com/region**

Cengage Learning products are represented in Canada by Nelson Education, Ltd.

For your course and learning solutions, visit **www.cengage.com.**
Purchase any of our products at your local college store
or at our preferred online store **www.cengagebrain.com.**

Printed in the United States of America
1 2 3 4 5 6 7 14 13 12 11 10

To the futures of Adam and Marisa, Lee, and Rachel Gerston
and
the memories of Anna and Teter Christensen and Tillie and Chester Welliever

Contents

Preface

When we published the first edition of *California Politics and Government: A Practical Approach* twenty years ago, we promised a book that emphasized the "nuts and bolts" of the state's political processes and institutions. We remain equally committed to that objective in this, our eleventh, edition. Within the complexities of cumbersome institutions, competing interests, and over-the-top personalities exists a state government responsible to a population of more than 38 million people. Our task then and our task today remains the same: to help explain how these two entities interact in the political collage otherwise known as California.

Our fascination grows with every edition. The more we observe California, the more we realize that the state doesn't fit any single neat pattern or formula. Rather, it is an awkward combination of historic traditions and contemporary extremes perched atop a wobbly governmental foundation of dysfunctional institutions. The more reformers attempt to pull the state's politics and policies in a new direction, the more vested interests protect their turfs by exercising a variety of strategies. Sometimes amazed, sometimes aghast, and often apathetic, Californians struggle to make sense of this perplexing picture.

Our ongoing effort is to clarify confusion—not an easy task, given California's composition. Some themes persist year after year with great certainty. Conflicts between the governor and legislature, Democrats and Republicans, and tax cutters and government boosters are standard fare. Other topics, such as immigration, gay rights, and education reform, sometimes clog the agenda, only to disappear until they reappear. Through it all, the state's policymakers struggle to meet ever-swelling needs with too few resources. All this takes place in a state where the "haves" and "have-nots" seem to grow farther apart each year. Still, California moves, even if the direction is tentative and the beat irregular.

All of which takes us to the eleventh edition. As with the past editions, we honor the timeless topics that have historically defined our reporting. We touch on institutions, their leaders, and issues that affect most of us one way or another.

Perennial themes such as gridlock, direct democracy, and contentious relations with the federal government receive attention because they are, well, perennial! At the same time, we flow with the action on current themes such as soaring interest group influence, the power of money, deteriorating infrastructure, and a state on the verge of bankruptcy.

Specifically, we focus on election changes in the executive and legislative branches, along with new appointments to the courts. We are also drawn to the growing fiscal crisis at the local government level, the soaring campaign contributions of interest groups, and the increasing power of the Latino vote in a state where racial and ethnic minorities now comprise a solid majority. In addition, we discuss the impact of the 2010 congressional elections; although the national Republican wave stopped at the Sierras, California's role in Washington was impacted greatly by the switch from Democratic to Republican control in the House of Representatives.

But just because we focus on these themes today doesn't mean the same combination of issues will persist tomorrow. Like the changes with a twist of a kaleidoscope, California is always on the move. Our challenge is to keep up and explain the state's many mysteries.

This book is an effort to move us along that path. Because we focus on nuts and bolts, we offer extended opportunities at the end of each chapter to explore topics through books and various Web sites online. We also include a Glossary that contains definitions of the key terms, offices, institutions, and events printed in bold throughout the book. Combined, these tools provide access to and elaboration about the many themes discussed in *California Politics and Government.*

Many have assisted us on our journey. Our friends in politics, elected office, and the media, as well as fellow academics, have provided valuable information and insights at numerous junctures. We would especially like to thank the following reviewers whose comments helped mold this edition: Maria Sampanis, California State University, Sacramento; Robert Melsh, Mt. San Jacinto College; Ted Lempert, University of California, Berkeley; and Alex Yamato, San José State University. Most of all, we continue to benefit from our students who, with their penetrating questions and thoughtful comments, push us to examine topics that we might not have considered otherwise. Some have themselves gone on to their own political careers and have made us equally proud.

Finally, we are indebted to the attentive production staff at Cengage, who artfully managed an incredibly tight schedule to facilitate production within weeks of the November 2, 2010, election. They include Carolyn Merrill, executive editor; Lydia LeStar, marketing manager; Susan Miscio, content project manager; and Charu Khanna of MPS Ltd. who patiently and efficiently worked with us from manuscript to page proofs. All these people and others helped us to complete this project to the best of our abilities. Of course, in the end we assume full responsibility for the product.

Larry N.Gerston
Terry Christensen
December 31, 2010

About the Authors

Larry N. Gerston professor of political science at San Jose State University, interacts with the political process as both an author and an observer. As an author, he has written nine academic books in addition to *California Politics and Government: A Practical Approach*, including *Making Public Policy: From Conflict to Resolution* (1983), *Politics in the Golden State* (with Terry Christensen, 1984), *The Deregulated Society* (with Cynthia Fraleigh and Robert Schwab, 1988), *American Government: Politics, Process and Policies* (1993), *Public Policy: Process and Principles* (1987), *Public Policymaking in a Democratic Society: A Guide to Civic Engagement* (2002), *Recall! California's Political Earthquake* (with Christensen, 2004), *American Federalism: A Concise Introduction* (2007), and *Confronting Reality: Ten Issues Threatening to Implode American Society and How We Can Fix It* (2009). On a lighter note, Gerston has written *The Costco Experience: An Unofficial Survivor's Guide* (2003). As an observer, Gerston serves as the political analyst for NBC11, a San Francisco Bay Area television station. He has written more than a hundred op-ed pieces for newspapers throughout the nation and appears regularly as a motivational speaker. Gerston is a consultant for the Center for Civic Education, where he frequently leads seminars for the Project Citizen public policy program.

Terry Christensen was named San Jose State University's Outstanding Professor in 1998. He has also won awards for his scholarship and his service to the university. He is the author or co-author of nine books and frequent newspaper op-ed pieces. Local and national media regularly call on him for analysis of politics in California and Silicon Valley. In addition to other books co-authored with Larry Gerston, his works include *Projecting Politics: Political Messages in American Films* (2005), co-authored by Peter Haas, and *Local Politics: A Practical Guide to Governing at the Grassroots* (2006), co-authored by Tom Hogen-Esch. Christensen is experienced in practical politics at the local level as an advocate of policy proposals, an adviser to grassroots groups, and an adviser and mentor to candidates for local office—many of whom are his former students. He has served on numerous civic committees and commissions. Most recently, he served as the founding executive director of CommUniverCity San Jose (www.communivercitysanjose.org), a partnership between the City of San Jose, San Jose State University, and adjacent neighborhoods. Through CommUniverCity, hundreds of students are learning about life and politics in their community through service projects selected by neighborhood residents and supported by the city.

1

California's People, Economy, and Politics: Yesterday, Today, and Tomorrow

CHAPTER CONTENTS

Is California a failed state? That term is usually applied to collapsed nation-states like Somalia—places that lack a cohesive central government and often are caught up in civil war. But after a decade of budget deficits and gridlock in the California state capital, many observers, including even California loyalists like historian Kevin Starr, were asking that question.[1] To many, California politics seems turbulent and unpredictable. Political leaders rise and fall precipitately. Wealthy candidates and special interests are accused of "buying" elections. The governor and the legislature can't agree on a budget on schedule, as a prolonged recession grips the economy. While state government stalls in gridlock, issues are referred to the voters, who are often confused by complex and sometimes obscure ballot measures. Some say this is democracy gone mad; others have concluded that California is ungovernable.

But however volatile or dysfunctional California politics may seem, it is serious business that affects us all, and it can be understood by examining the history and present characteristics of our state—especially its changing population and economy. Wave after wave of immigrants have made California a diverse, multicultural society, while new technologies repeatedly transform the state's economy. The resulting disparate demographic and economic interests compete for the benefits and protections conferred by government and thus shape the state's politics. To understand California today—and tomorrow—we need to know a little about its past and about the development of the competing interests within the state.

COLONIZATION, REBELLION, AND STATEHOOD

The first Californians probably were immigrants like the rest of us who followed. Archaeologists believe that the ancestors of American Indians crossed an ice or land bridge or traveled by sea from Asia to Alaska thousands of years ago and then headed south. Europeans began exploring the California coast in the early 1500s, but colonization didn't start until 1769, when the Spanish established a string of missions and military outposts. About 300,000 Native Americans were living here then, mostly near the coast.

These native Californians were brought to the missions as Catholic converts and workers, but European diseases and the destruction of the native culture reduced their numbers to about 100,000 by 1849. Disease and massacres wiped out entire tribes, and the Indian population continued to diminish throughout the nineteenth century. Today, less than 1 percent of California's population is Native American, and many feel alienated from a society that has overwhelmed their peoples, cultures, and traditions. Chronic poverty, however, has been alleviated for some by the development of casinos on native lands, a phenomenon that has also made some tribes major players in state politics.

Apart from building missions, the Spaniards did little to develop their faraway possession. Not much changed when Mexico, which included California within its boundaries, declared its independence from Spain in 1822. A few thousand Mexicans quietly raised cattle on vast ranches and continued to build the province's small towns around their central plazas.

Meanwhile, expansionist interests in the United States coveted California's rich lands and access to the Pacific Ocean. When Mexico and the United States went to war over Texas in 1846, Yankee immigrants to California seized the moment and declared independence from Mexico. After the U.S. victory, Mexico surrendered its claim to lands extending from Texas to California. By this time, foreigners already outnumbered Californians of Spanish ancestry 9,000 to 7,500.

In 1848 gold was discovered, and the '49ers who started arriving the next year brought the nonnative population to 264,000 by 1852. Many immigrants came directly from Europe. The first Chinese people also arrived to work in the mines, which yielded more than a billion dollars' worth of gold in five years.

The surge in population and commerce moved the new Californians to political action. A constitutional convention consisting of forty-eight delegates (only seven of whom were native Californians) threw together the **Constitution of 1849** by cutting and pasting from the constitutions of existing states; the convention requested statehood, which the U.S. Congress quickly granted. The constitutional structure of the new state was remarkably similar to what we have today, with a two-house legislature; a supreme court; and an executive branch consisting of a governor, lieutenant governor, controller, attorney general, and superintendent of public instruction. The constitution also included a bill of rights, but only white males were allowed to vote. California's Chinese, African American, and Native American residents were soon prohibited by law from owning land, testifying in court, or attending public schools.

The voters approved the constitution, and San Jose became the first state capital. With housing in short supply, many newly elected legislators had to lodge in tents, and the primitive living conditions were exacerbated by heavy rain and flooding. Despite these conditions, the partying politicians became known—and discredited—as "the legislature of a thousand drinks." The state capital soon moved on to Vallejo and Benicia, finally settling in 1854 in Sacramento—closer to the gold fields.

As the gold rush ended, a land rush began. While small homesteads were common in other states because of federal ownership of land, much of California had been divided into huge tracts by Spanish and Mexican land grants. As early as 1870, a few hundred men owned most of the farmland. Their ranches were the forerunners of the agribusiness corporations of today, and as the mainstay of the state's economy, they exercised even more clout than their modern successors.

In less than fifty years, California had belonged to three different nations. During the same period, its economy and population had changed dramatically as hundreds of thousands of immigrants from all over the world came to claim their share of the "Golden State." The pattern of a rapidly evolving, multicultural polity was set.

RAILROADS, MACHINES, AND REFORM

Technology wrought the next transformation in the form of railroads. In 1861 Sacramento merchants Charles Crocker, Mark Hopkins, Collis Huntington, and Leland Stanford founded the railroad that would become the **Southern Pacific Railroad**. They persuaded Congress to provide millions of dollars in land grants and loan subsidies for a railroad linking California with the eastern United States, thus greatly expanding the market for California's products. Stanford, then governor, used his influence to provide state assistance. Cities and counties also contributed—under the threat of being bypassed by the railroad. To obtain workers at cheap rates, the railroad builders imported 15,000 Chinese laborers.

When the transcontinental track was completed in 1869, the Southern Pacific expanded its system throughout the state by building new lines and buying up existing ones. The railroad crushed competitors by cutting its shipping charges, and by the 1880s it had become the state's dominant transportation company, as well as its largest private landowner, in possession of 11 percent of the entire state. With its business agents doubling as political representatives in almost every California city and county, the Southern Pacific soon developed a formidable political machine. "The Octopus," as novelist Frank Norris called the railroad, placed allies in state and local offices through its control of both the Republican and Democratic parties. Once there, these officials protected the interests of the Southern Pacific if they wanted to continue in office. County tax assessors who were supported by the political machine set favorable tax rates for the railroad and its allies, while the machine-controlled legislature ensured a hands-off policy by state government.

THE WORKINGMEN'S PARTY

People in small towns and rural areas who were unwilling to support the machine lost jobs, business, and other benefits. Some moved to cities, especially San Francisco, where manufacturing jobs were available. Chinese workers who had been brought to California to build the railroad also sought work in the cities when it was completed. But when a depression in the 1870s made jobs scarce, these newcomers faced hostile treatment from earlier immigrants. Led by Denis Kearney, Irish immigrants became the core of the **Workingmen's Party**, a political organization that blamed economic difficulties on the railroad and the Chinese.

Small farmers who opposed the railroad united through the Grange movement. In 1879 the Grangers and the Workingmen's Party called California's second constitutional convention in hopes of breaking the railroad's hold on the state. The **Constitution of 1879** mandated regulation of railroads, utilities, banks, and other corporations. An elected State Board of Equalization was set up to ensure the fairness of local tax assessments on railroads and their friends, as well as their enemies. The new constitution also prohibited the Chinese from owning land, voting, or working for state or local government.

The railroad soon reclaimed power, however, gaining control of the very agencies that were created to regulate it. Nonetheless, the efforts made during this period to regulate big business and control racial relations became recurring themes in California life and politics, and much of the Constitution of 1879 remains intact today.

THE PROGRESSIVES

The growth fostered by the railroad eventually produced a new middle class, encompassing merchants, doctors, lawyers, teachers, and skilled workers, who were not dependent on the railroad. They objected to the corrupt practices and favoritism of the railroad's political machine, which they thought was restraining economic development in their communities. The new middle class demanded honesty and competence, which they called "good government." In 1907 a number of these crusaders established the Lincoln-Roosevelt League, a reform group within the Republican Party, and became part of the national Progressive movement. Their leader, Hiram Johnson, was elected governor in 1910; they also captured control of the state legislature.

To break the power of the machine, the **Progressives** introduced a wave of reforms that shape California politics to this day. Predictably, they created a new regulatory agency for the railroads and utilities, the Public Utilities Commission (PUC). Most of their reforms, however, aimed at weakening the political parties as tools of bosses and machines. Instead of party bosses handpicking candidates at party conventions, the voters now were given the power to select their party's nominees for office in primary elections. Cross-filing further diluted party power by allowing candidates to file for and win the nominations of more than one political party. The Progressives made city and county elections "nonpartisan" by removing party labels from local ballots altogether. They also created a civil service system to select state employees on the basis of their qualifications rather than their political connections.

Finally, the Progressives introduced direct democracy, which allowed the voters to amend the constitution and create laws through initiatives and referenda and to recall, or remove, elected officials before their terms expired. Supporters of an initiative, referendum, or recall must circulate petitions and collect a specified number of signatures of registered voters before it becomes a ballot measure or proposition.

Like the Workingmen's Party before them, the Progressives were concerned about immigration. Antagonism toward recent Japanese immigrants (who numbered 72,000 by 1910) resulted in Progressive support for a ban on land ownership by aliens and the National Immigration Act of 1924, which effectively halted Asian immigration. Other, more positive changes by the Progressives included giving women the right to vote, passing child labor and workers' compensation laws, and implementing conservation programs to protect natural resources.

Thanks largely to the Progressive reforms, the railroad's political machine eventually died; California's increasingly diverse economy had also weakened the machine, however, as the emerging oil, automobile, and trucking industries gave the state alternative means of transportation and shipping. These and other growing industries ultimately restructured economic and political power in California.

The reform movement waned in the 1920s, but the Progressive legacy of weak political parties and direct democracy opened up California's politics to its citizens, as well as to powerful interest groups and individual candidates with strong personalities. A long and detailed constitution is also part of the legacy. The Progressives instituted their reforms by amending (and thus lengthening) the Constitution of 1879 rather than calling for a new constitutional convention.

Direct democracy subsequently enabled voters and interest groups to amend the constitution, which has become an extraordinarily lengthy document over time.

THE GREAT DEPRESSION AND WORLD WAR II

California's population grew by more than 2 million in the 1920s (see Table 1.1). Most of the newcomers headed for Los Angeles, where employment opportunities in shipping, filmmaking, and manufacturing (of clothing, automobiles, and aircraft) abounded. Then came the Great Depression of the 1930s, which saw the unemployment rate soar from 3 percent in 1925 to 33 percent by 1933. Even so, more than a million people still came to California, including thousands of poor white immigrants from the "dust bowl" of the drought-impacted Midwest. Many wandered through California's great Central Valley in search of work, displacing Mexicans—who earlier had supplanted the Chinese and Japanese—as the state's farm workers. Racial antagonism ran high, and many Mexicans were arbitrarily sent back to Mexico. Labor unrest reached a crescendo in the early 1930s, as workers on farms, in canneries, and on the docks of San Francisco and Los Angeles fought for higher wages and an eight-hour workday.

The immigrants and union activists of the 1920s and 1930s also changed California politics. Many registered as Democrats, thus challenging the dominant Republicans. The Depression and President Franklin Roosevelt's popular New Deal helped the Democrats become California's majority party in registration, although winning elections proved more difficult. Their biggest boost came from Upton Sinclair, a novelist, a socialist, and the Democratic candidate for governor in 1934.

**T A B L E 1.1 California's Population Growth,
Selected Decades, 1850–2010**

Year	Population	Percentage of U.S. Population
1850	93,000	0.4
1900	1,485,000	2.0
1950	10,643,000	7.0
1960	15,863,000	8.8
1970	20,039,000	9.8
1980	23,780,000	10.5
1990	29,733,000	11.7
2000	33,871,648	12.0
2010	38,648,090	12.6

SOURCE: California Department of Finance and U.S. Census.

Sinclair's End Poverty in California (EPIC) movement almost led to an election victory, but the state's conservative establishment spent an unprecedented $10 million to defeat him. The Democrats finally gained the governorship in 1938, but their candidate, Culbert Olson, was the only Democratic winner between 1894 and 1958.

World War II revived the economic boom. The federal government spent $35 billion in California between 1940 and 1946, creating 500,000 jobs in defense industries. California's radio, electronics, and aircraft industries grew at phenomenal rates. The jobs brought new immigrants, including many African Americans, whose proportion of the state's population quadrupled during the 1940s. African Americans were nevertheless on the periphery of the state's racial conflicts—unlike Japanese and Mexican Americans. During the war, more than 100,000 Japanese Americans, suspected of loyalty to their ancestral homeland, were sent to prison camps (officially called internment centers). Antagonism toward Mexican Americans resulted in the Zoot Suit Riots in Los Angeles in 1943, when Anglo sailors and police attacked Mexican Americans wearing distinctive suits featuring long jackets with wide lapels, padded shoulders, and high-waisted, pegged pants.

While the cities boomed, with defense industries becoming permanent fixtures and aerospace and electronics adding to the momentum, the Central Valley bloomed, thanks to water projects initiated by the state and federal governments during the 1930s. Dams and canals brought water to the desert and reaffirmed agriculture as a mainstay of California's economy.

Although the voters chose a Democratic governor during the Great Depression, they returned to the Republican fold as the economy revived. Earl Warren, one of a new breed of moderate, urbane Republicans, was elected governor in 1942, 1946, and 1950, becoming the only individual to win the office three times until Jerry Brown was elected in 2010. Warren used cross-filing to win the nominations of both parties and staked out a relationship with the voters that he claimed was above party politics. A classic example of California's personality-oriented politics, Warren left the state in 1953 to become chief justice of the United States Supreme Court.

GROWTH, CHANGE, AND POLITICAL TURMOIL

In 1958 the Republican Party was in disarray because of infighting. Californians elected a Democratic governor, Edmund G. "Pat" Brown, and a Democratic majority in the state legislature. To prevent Republicans from taking advantage of cross-filing again, the state's new leaders immediately outlawed that electoral device.

In control of both the governor's office and the legislature for the first time in the twentieth century, Democrats moved aggressively to develop the state's infrastructure. Completion of the massive California Water Project, construction of the state highway network, and creation of an unparalleled higher education system were among the advances to accommodate a growing population.

Meanwhile, in the 1960s, California's black and Latino minorities became more assertive, pushing for civil rights, desegregation of schools, access to higher education, and improved treatment for California's predominantly Latino farm workers.

The demands of minority groups alienated some white voters, however, and the Democratic programs were expensive. After opening their purse strings during the eight-year tenure of Pat Brown, Californians became more cautious about the state's direction. Race riots precipitated by police brutality in Los Angeles, along with student unrest over the Vietnam War, also turned the voters against liberal Democrats such as Brown.

In 1966 Republican Ronald Reagan was elected governor; he moved the state in a more conservative direction before going on to serve as president. His successor as governor, Democrat Edmund G. "Jerry" Brown, Jr., was the son of the earlier governor Brown and a liberal on social issues. Like Reagan, however, the younger Brown led California away from spending on growth-inducing infrastructure, such as highways and schools. In 1978 the voters solidified this change with the watershed tax-cutting initiative, Proposition 13 (see Chapter 8). Although Democrats have long outnumbered Republicans among California's registered voters, Brown was followed by Republicans George Deukmejian in 1982 and Pete Wilson in 1990, each of whom served two terms in office.

In 1998 California elected Gray Davis, its first Democratic governor in sixteen years. He was reelected in 2002 despite voter concerns about an energy crisis, a recession, and a growing budget deficit. As a consequence of these crises and what some perceived as an arrogant attitude, Davis faced an unprecedented recall election in October 2003. The voters removed him from office and replaced him with Republican Arnold Schwarzenegger, who was reelected in 2006.

In 2010, former governor Jerry Brown attempted a comeback and made history as California's youngest and oldest governor when he defeated former eBay chief executive Meg Whitman, a Republican who broke the U.S. campaign spending record for any office other than the presidency.

Democrats have had more consistent success in the state legislature and the congressional delegation, where they have been the dominant party since 1960. California voters have also opted for Democrats in every presidential election since 1988.

The challenges of governing California have been exacerbated by recurring conflicts between a Democratic legislature and Republican governors, as well as by the constitutional requirement for a supermajority to enact the state budget. Meanwhile, the voters have become increasingly involved in policymaking by initiative and referendum (see Chapter 2). Amendments to California's constitution, which require voter approval, appear on almost every state ballot. As a consequence, California's Constitution of 1879 has been amended over five hundred times; the U.S. Constitution includes just twenty-seven amendments.

Throughout these changes the state's population continued to grow, outpacing most other states so much that the California delegation to the U.S. House of Representatives now numbers fifty-three—more than twenty-one other states combined. Much of this growth was the result of a new wave of immigration facilitated by more flexible national immigration laws during the 1960s and 1970s. Immigration from Asia—especially from Southeast Asia after the Vietnam War—increased greatly. A national amnesty for undocumented residents also enabled many Mexicans to gain citizenship and bring their families from Mexico. In all, 85 percent of the 6 million newcomers and births in California in the 1980s were Asian, Latino, or black. Growth slowed in the 1990s, as 2 million more people left the state than came to it from other states, but California's population continued to increase as a result of births and immigration from abroad. In 1990 whites made up 57 percent of the state's population; by 2000 they were 47 percent.

Constantly increasing diversity enlivened California's culture and provided a steady flow of new workers, but it also increased tensions. Some affluent Californians retreated to gated communities; others fled the state. Racial conflict broke out between gangs on the streets and in prisons. As in difficult economic times throughout California's history, a recession during the early 1990s led many Californians, including Governor Wilson, to blame immigrants, especially those who were in California illegally. A series of ballot measures raised divisive race-related issues such as illegal immigration, bilingualism, and affirmative action. The issue of immigration enflames California politics to this day, although the increasing electoral clout of minorities and big public demonstrations in support of immigrants have provided some balance.

CALIFORNIA TODAY

If California were an independent nation, its economy would rank eighth in the world, with an annual gross national product exceeding $1.8 trillion. Much of the state's strength stems from its economic diversity (see Table 1.2). The elements of this diversity also constitute powerful political interests in state politics.

Half of California—mostly desert and mountains—is owned by the state and federal governments. In the rural areas, a few big farm corporations control much of the state's rich farmlands. These enormous corporate farms, known as agribusinesses, make California the nation's leading farm state, producing more than four hundred crops and providing nearly half of the vegetables, fruits, and nuts and a quarter of the dairy products consumed nationally. Grapes and wine are also top products, with 4,600 growers and 2,843 wineries.

State politics affects this huge economic force in many ways, but most notably in labor relations, environmental regulation, and water supply. Farmers and their employees have battled for decades over issues ranging from wages to safety. Under the leadership of Cesar Chavez and the United Farm Workers union, laborers organized. Supported by public boycotts of certain farm products, they achieved some improvements in working conditions, but the struggle continues today. California's agricultural industry is also caught up in environmental

T A B L E 1.2 California's Economy

Industrial Sector	Employees	Amount (in millions)
Professional and business services	2,035,300	$ 260,133
Education and health services	1,766,600	131,067
Leisure and hospitality services	1,483,600	75,639
Other services	477,300	42,196
Information	447,600	112,752
Government	2,482,000	216,764
Trade, transportation, and utilities	2,580,100	299,645
Manufacturing	1,237,200	181,134
Finance, insurance, and real estate	777,800	416,324
Construction	553,800	67,770
Mining and natural resources	24,700	43,333
Agriculture	389,100	36,600
Total, all sectors	14,255,100	$1,883,357

SOURCE: California Employment Development Department, www.edd.ca.gov (accessed May 2010); and U.S. Department of Commerce, Bureau of Economic Analysis, *Survey of Current Business,* June 2010.

issues, including the use of pesticides and the pollution of water supplies. In addition, booming growth in the Central Valley has urbanized some farmland, bringing "city" problems such as traffic and crowded schools to once-rural areas. The biggest issue, however, is always water. Most of California's cities and farmlands must import water from other parts of the state. Thanks to government subsidies, farmers claim 80 percent of the state's water supply at prices so low that they have little reason to improve inefficient irrigation systems. Meanwhile, the growth of urban areas is limited by their water supplies. Today, agriculture is in the thick of California politics as the state strives to balance an essential and powerful industry with the interests of its other citizens.

Agriculture is big business, but many more Californians work in manufacturing, especially in the aerospace, defense, and high-tech industries. Employment in manufacturing, however, has been declining in California for some years, especially after the federal government reduced military and defense spending in the 1990s when the collapse of communism in the Soviet Union brought an end to the Cold War. Employment in California shifted to postindustrial occupations such as retail sales, tourism, and services, although jobs in these sectors often pay low wages. Government policies on growth, the environment, and taxation affect all of these employment sectors, and all suffer when any one sector goes into a slump.

But the salvation of California's economy is its innovation, especially in telecommunications, entertainment, medical equipment, international trade, and above all, high-tech businesses spawned by the defense and aerospace companies that withered in the early 1990s. At the peak of the high-tech boom, California hosted one-fourth of the nation's high-tech firms, which provided nearly a million jobs.

Half of the nation's computer engineers worked in **Silicon Valley**, named after the silicon chip that revolutionized the computer industry. Running between San Jose and San Francisco, Silicon Valley became a center for innovation in technology from technical instruments, computer chips, networking equipment, workstations, and software to Internet-based dot-com businesses. Biomedical and pharmaceutical companies also proliferated, further contributing to California's transformation.

Computer technology also spurred rapid expansion of the entertainment industry, long a key component of California's economy. This growth particularly benefited the Los Angeles area, which had been hit hard by cuts in defense spending. Together, entertainment and tourism provide more than 500,000 jobs for Californians. Half of these are in film and television, but tourism remains a bastion of the economy, with California regularly ranking first among the states in visitors. Along with agriculture, high-tech, telecommunications, and other industries, these businesses have made California a leader in both international and domestic trade. All these industries are part of a globalized economy, which has bolstered and sustained California's economy. Much of this trade goes through the massive port complex of Los Angeles/Long Beach, as well as the San Francisco Bay Port of Oakland; much is also shipped by air.

The California economy has been on a roller coaster for the past few years, though. It has been in and out of recession—first in the early 1990s, and then again after the terrible events of September 11, 2001, when the California-centered Internet boom went bust as thousands of dot-com companies failed to generate projected profits. High-tech industry went into decline, and tens of thousands of workers lost their jobs, some of which were "off-shored" (moved to other countries). At about the same time, an energy crisis hit California. The state had deregulated energy suppliers in 1996 at the urging of industry, but by 2000, prices for gas and electricity had risen and parts of the state experienced shortages of electrical power. Belatedly, Governor Davis took action to resolve the crisis, but his initial caution and the exorbitant prices the state paid to ensure supplies caused his popularity to slump. All these factors combined to push California into a recession, with unemployment reaching 7 percent statewide and 9 percent in Silicon Valley in 2003 (the national rate was 5.9 percent).

When tax revenues rose during the heady days of the dot-coms, Governor Davis and the legislature had expanded programs and cut some fees and taxes. But when the boom ended, tax revenues declined precipitously, producing a state budget deficit that ultimately exceeded $30 billion. The deficit and other issues plunged California into a crisis that continued beyond the recall of Governor Davis in 2003. After a brief resurgence in 2006–2007, California's economy slipped back toward recession as unemployment reached 12.4 percent in 2010 (the U.S. rate was 9.7 percent). California had lost hundreds of thousands of manufacturing jobs since the 1990s as employers migrated to other states. By 2010, however, employment in all sectors, even film and television production, was in decline. The national home finance and foreclosure crisis also hit the California housing market and construction industry hard. Governor Schwarzenegger found himself faced with even bigger budget deficits than his predecessor—and nearly the same low public approval ratings.

Throughout its history, California has experienced economic ups and downs like these, recovered, reinvented itself, and moved on thanks to the diversity of its economy and its people and their ability to adapt to change. While some businesses have forsaken California for other states, complaining of burdensome regulation and the high cost of doing business in California, the Public Policy Institute of California reports that the skill and higher productivity of the state's workforce, access to capital, and quality of life compensate for such costs and keep the state attractive to many businesses.[2] Innovation continues to be an economic mainstay as well. Nanotechnology companies, for example, are concentrated in the San Francisco Bay Area, while biotechnology thrives in the San Diego region and green industry (for example, solar power and electric cars) booms throughout California. Small businesses—many of which are minority owned—form the backbone of the California economy, and while many struggle, others thrive. Most other states lack these advantages; some are dependent on a single industry or product, and none can match the energy and optimism brought by California's constant flow of immigrants eager to take jobs in the state's new and old industries.

California's globalized economy consistently attracts more immigrants than any other state; as of 2010, 26.6 percent of the state's population was foreign born, down slightly from a peak of 27.4 percent in 2007.[3] For perspective, the foreign-born share of the U.S. population was 12.2 percent. Fifty-six percent of California's immigrants are from Latin America (mostly Mexico), and 34 percent are from Asia (especially the Philippines, China, Vietnam, India, and Korea). Significantly for the California economy, 75 percent of the state's immigrant population is of working age (twenty-five to sixty-four).[4] An estimated 3 million immigrants are in California illegally. As a consequence of so much immigration, nearly 40 percent of all Californians over the age of five speak a language other than English at home, resulting in a major challenge for California schools. As in past centuries, immigration and language have been hot-button political issues in California in recent years.

The extent of California's ethnic diversity is indicated in Table 1.3. Although non-Latino whites remain the single largest group, they are no longer a majority. Overall, the black and white proportions of California's population have decreased, while Asian and Latino numbers have grown rapidly since the 1970s, slowly producing a shift in political power. As of 2008, 70.6 percent of students in California's public schools were nonwhite.[5]

The realization of the California dream is not shared equally among these groups. Although the median household income as of 2009 was $58,931 according the U.S. Census Bureau, the income of 15.3 percent of Californians fell below the federal poverty level—slightly above the national average—but the state's rate is considerably higher when the cost of living in California is factored in. Over half the students in California schools qualify for free or reduced-price meals.[6] The gap between rich and poor in California is among the largest in the United States and is still growing. Poverty is worst among Latinos, blacks, and Southeast Asians, who tend to hold low-paying service jobs; other Asians, along with Anglos, predominate in the more comfortable professional classes.

T A B L E 1.3 California's Racial and Ethnic Diversity

	1990	2000	2010
Non-Latino white	57.1%	47.3%	42.0%
Latino	26.0	32.4	37.1
Asian/Pacific Islander	9.2	11.4	12.4
Black	7.1	6.5	5.8
Native American	0.6	0.5	0.6
Mixed race	N.A.	1.9	2.1

SOURCE: U.S. Census; California Department of Finance, *Population Projections by Race/Ethnicity for California and Its Counties, 2000–2050,* www.dof.ca.gov (accessed June 18, 2010).

As the poor grow in number, some observers fear that California's middle class is vanishing. Once a majority, many of the middle class have slipped down the economic ladder, and others have simply fled the state. Instead of a class structure with a great bulge in the center, California now exhibits an "**hourglass economy**," with many people doing very well at the top, many barely getting by at the bottom, and fewer and fewer in the middle. Recent growth has concentrated in low- and high-wage jobs, and the income gap continues to widen.[7]

The costs of housing and health care are at the heart of this problem. The housing crisis of 2008–2010 increased the affordability of home ownership for some families, but many more suffered substantial losses of equity in their homes, and some lost their homes to foreclosure. With a median home price of $306,230 in 2010 compared with the U.S. median of $175,000, Californians still spent more of their income on housing than the national average, and fewer families were able to afford to own homes, especially in the coastal counties from San Diego to San Francisco. Homes were more affordable in inland California, however.[8] Overall, home ownership in California lags well behind the national average, especially for Latinos and blacks. Health care is also a problem for poor and working Californians. Over 24 percent (8.2 million) have no health insurance,[9] although coverage for children was expanded under the state's Healthy Families program established in 2001.

Geographic divisions complicate California's economic and ethnic diversity. In the past, the most pronounced of these divisions was between the northern and southern portions of the state. The San Francisco Bay Area tended to be diverse, liberal, and in elections, Democratic, while Southern California was staunchly Republican and much less diverse. However, with growth and greater diversity, Los Angeles also began voting Democratic. Today, the greatest division is between the coastal and inland regions of the state (see Figure 2-3). Democrats now outnumber Republicans in San Diego, for example, and even notoriously conservative Orange County has elected a Latina Democrat to Congress.

But even as the differences between northern and southern California fade, the contrast between coastal and inland California has increased.[10] The state's vast Central Valley has led the way in population and job growth, with cities from Sacramento to Fresno to Bakersfield gobbling up farmland. The Inland Empire, from Riverside to San Bernardino, has grown even more rapidly since the late 1990s. Although still sparsely populated, California's northern coast, Sierra Nevada, and southern desert regions are also growing, while retaining their own distinct identities. Water, agriculture, and the environment are major issues in all these areas. Except for Sacramento, inland California is more conservative than the coastal region of the state. Perhaps ironically, a recent study showed that the liberal counties of the coast contribute more per capita in state taxes, and the conservative inland counties receive more per capita for social service programs.[11] While coastal California remains politically dominant, the impact of inland areas on California politics increases with every election.

CALIFORNIA'S PEOPLE, ECONOMY, AND POLITICS

All these elements of California's economic, demographic, and geographic diversity vie with one another for political influence in the context of political structures that were created more than a hundred years ago. Dissatisfaction with this system has resulted in dozens of reforms by ballot measure, a recall election, and more recently, calls for a constitutional convention. Voter frustration is at a peak. As of 2010, only 18 percent of Californians felt the state was "going in the right direction" (compared with 55 percent in 2007); only 23 percent approved of the governor's performance (compared with 57 percent in 2007); and 16 percent approved of the performance of the legislature (compared with 41 percent in 2007).[12] Perhaps people see California as a failed state, or maybe they're just frustrated with the current leadership. A majority, however, support constitutional reform,[13] which could be done piecemeal through ballot measures or more comprehensively through a constitutional convention. A convention can be proposed by a two-thirds vote of the state legislature (which some consider unlikely) and then approved by the voters. In the chapters that follow, we'll see how the diverse interests of our state operate in the current political system and gain an understanding of how it all works, why voters and others may feel frustration, and what some are doing to bring about change even as others resist.

NOTES

1. Quoted in Paul Harris, "Will California Become America's First Failed State?" *Guardian.co.uk,* October 5, 2009, www.guardian.co.uk/world/2009/oct/04/california-failing-state-debt (accessed June 14, 2010). See also www.newsweek.com/2010/01/25/california-america-s-first-failed-state.html (accessed June 14, 2010). Googling "California as a failed state" produces 2,870,000 hits.

2. Jed Kolko, "California Economy: Planning for a Better Future," July 2009, www.ppic.org (accessed June 18, 2010).

3. USC Population Dynamics Research Group, School of Policy, Planning and Development, "The New Place of Birth Profile of Los Angeles and California Residents in 2010," www.usc.edu/schools/sppd/research/popdynamics/futures (accessed June 18, 2010).

4. Public Policy Institute of California, "Just the Facts: Immigrants in California," June 2008, www.ppic.org (accessed June 21, 2010).

5. Southern Education Foundation, January 31, 2010, www.southerneducation.org/pdf/New%20Diverse%20Majority-Summary.pdf (accessed June 21, 2010).

6. *Ibid.*

7. California Budget Project, "A Generation of Widening Inequality," August 2007, www.cpb.org (accessed June 21, 2010); and California Budget Project, "Policy Points: New Data Show That California's Income Gaps Continue to Widen," June 2009, www.cpb.org (accessed June 21, 2010).

8. For information about regional variation in housing costs, see the National Association of Home Builders (NAHB)/Wells Fargo Housing Opportunity Index (HOI), www.nahb.org/reference_list.aspx?sectionID=135 (accessed June 13, 2010).

9. UCLA Center for Health and Policy Research, reported in "The Uninsured," *San Jose Mercury News,* March 17, 2010, p. A1.

10. See Frederick Douzet and Kenneth P. Miller, "California's East-West Divide," in *The New Political Geography of California,* ed. Frederick Douzet, Thad Kousser, and Kenneth P. Miller (Berkeley: Berkeley Public Policy Press, Institute of Governmental Studies, University of California, 2008).

11. Report from the Legislative Analyst's Office cited in "California's Unequal Give and Take," *San Jose Mercury News,* June 21, 2010.

12. Public Policy Institute of California, "Statewide Survey Time Trends," www.ppic.org (accessed June 21, 2010).

13. Public Policy Institute of California, "Statewide Survey," September 9, 2009. Thirty-three percent supported major constitutional change, 36 percent supported minor changes, 24 percent thought California's constitution was fine as is, and 7 percent don't know.

LEARN MORE ON THE WEB

The California Constitution:
www.leginfo.ca.gov/const-toc.html

Events and personalities from California's past at the California Historical Society's online historical guide:
www.californiahistoricalsociety.org/timeline

Demographic data:
www.dof.ca.gov/research/demographic

Demographic and business comparisons between California and the United States:
www.quickfacts.census.gov/qfd/states/06000.html
quickfacts.census.gov/qfd

Digitized photographs, documents, newspapers, political cartoons, works of art, diaries, oral histories, advertising, and other cultural artifacts:
www.calisphere.universityofcalifornia.edu

LEARN MORE AT THE LIBRARY

Sandra Bass and Bruce M. Cain, eds. *Racial and Ethnic Politics in California*. Berkeley: Berkeley Public Policy Press, Institute of Governmental Studies, University of California, 2008.

Frederick Douzet, Thad Kousser, and Kenneth P. Miller, eds. *The New Political Geography of California*. Berkeley: Berkeley Public Policy Press, Institute of Governmental Studies, University of California, 2008.

Carey McWilliams. *California: The Great Exception*. Berkeley: University of California Press, 1949.

Frank Norris. *The Octopus*. New York: Penguin, 1901. A novel of nineteenth-century California.

Peter Schrag. *California: America's High-Stakes Experiment*. Berkeley: University of California Press, 2006. Especially good on the impact of immigration.

Kevin Starr. *California: A History*. New York: Modern Library, 2005.

2

California's Political Parties and Direct Democracy

CHAPTER CONTENTS

In many states, political parties are strong organizations that control the selection of their nominees for public office, set out policy agendas based on their political ideologies, and can count on the loyalty of their voters. They link citizens to government, building coalitions of different interests and helping candidates make their case to the voters. This doesn't always happen in California, where party organizations are weak and voters make policy through the initiative process. As we'll learn in Chapter 5, political parties and party discipline are strong in the California state legislature, but that's not usually true of local or statewide party organizations. History tells us why: the Progressive reformers intentionally weakened political parties in order to rid California of the railroad-dominated political machine. In doing so, they unintentionally made candidate personalities, media manipulation, and fat campaign war chests as important in elections as political parties—and sometimes more so.

The Progressives also introduced **direct democracy**. Through the initiative, referendum, and recall, California voters gained the power to make law and even to overrule elected officials or remove them between elections. The reformers' intent was to empower citizens, but in practice, interest groups and politicians are more likely to use—and sometimes abuse—direct democracy.

Weak party organizations and direct democracy are fixtures of the state constitution and modern California politics. Some political observers argue that this combination promotes political disarray, governmental gridlock, and voters who are confused or turned off. Others believe that the system reflects a body of political values that eschews structured authority and maximizes opportunities for democratic decision making.

THE PROGRESSIVE LEGACY

To challenge the dominance of the Southern Pacific Railroad's political machine, Progressive reformers from both the Democratic and Republican parties focused on the machine's control of party conventions, where party leaders picked their candidates for various offices. Republican reformers scored the first breakthrough in 1908, when they succeeded in electing many antirailroad candidates to the state legislature. In 1909 the reform legislators replaced party conventions with **primary elections**, in which the registered voters of each party choose the nominee. Candidates who win their party's primary in these elections face the nominees of other parties in the November **general elections**. By instituting this system, the reformers ended the machine's control of the nomination process.

In 1910 Progressives won elections for both governor and the legislature. They introduced direct democracy to give policymaking authority to the people. They also replaced the party column ballot—which had permitted bloc voting for all the candidates of a single party by making just one mark—with separate balloting for each office. In addition, Progressive reformers introduced **cross-filing**, which permitted candidates of one party to seek the nominations of rival parties. Finally, the Progressives instituted **nonpartisan elections**, which eliminated party labels in contests to elect judges, school board members, and local government officials.

These changes reduced the railroad's control of the political parties, but they also sapped the strength of the party organizations. By allowing the voters to circumvent an unresponsive legislature, direct democracy paved the way for interest groups to dominate policymaking. Deletion of the party column ballot encouraged voters to cast their ballots for members of different parties for different offices (split-ticket voting), increasing the likelihood of a divided-party government (see Chapter 7). Nonpartisan local elections made it difficult for the parties to build their organizations at the grassroots level as well.

Party leaders tried to regain control of nominations by settling on favored candidates before the primary elections. Ultimately, however, such **preprimary endorsements** were also outlawed. Then in 1959, when Democrats gained control of the legislature for the first time in more than forty years, they outlawed cross-filing, which had been disproportionately helpful to Republican incumbents. This marked a return to the system in which candidates file for nomination for their own party only.

PARTY ORGANIZATION—STRUCTURE AND SUPPORTERS

Thanks to the Progressive reforms, political parties in California operate under unusual constraints. Although the original reformers have long since departed from the scene, the reform mentality remains very much a part of California's political culture.

Official Party Structures

According to the California State Elections Code, political parties can place candidates on the ballot by registering a number of members equal to 1 percent of the state vote in the most recent gubernatorial election or by submitting a petition with signatures amounting to 10 percent of that vote. After a party is qualified, if it retains the registration of at least 1 percent of the voters or if at least one of its candidates for any statewide office receives 2 percent of the votes cast, that party will be on the ballot in the next election. By virtue of their sizes, the Democratic and Republican parties have been fixtures on the ballot almost since statehood.

Minor parties, sometimes called **third parties**, are another story. Some have been on the ballot for decades; others have had brief political lives. In the 2006 general election, the Green, Libertarian, and Peace and Freedom parties each secured the minimum 2 percent of the vote for one of their statewide candidates, guaranteeing them positions on the ballot in 2010. No statewide candidates for the American Independent Party reached the 2 percent threshold, but enough voters are registered as American Independents to keep the party on the ballot. The total number of parties qualified for the 2010 California ballot, including Democrats and Republicans, is six.

Nonetheless, breaking the hold of the two major political parties has proved difficult. The Democratic and Republican candidates for governor garnered 95 percent of the vote in 2010—slightly less than the 98.2 percent shared by the Democratic and Republican candidates for president in 2008. Among the smaller parties, the Greens have been the most successful at winning elections. They have earned one seat in the state legislature and several seats at the local level.

California voters choose their party when they register to vote, which must be done fifteen or more days before the election. In 2010, 75.2 percent were registered as either Democrats or Republicans, 4.6 percent signed up with the

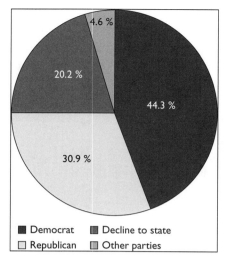

4.6 %

20.2 %

44.3 %

30.9 %

- ■ Democrat   ■ Decline to state
- □ Republican   ▨ Other parties

FIGURE 2.1 Party Registration in California, 2010. (Courtesy of Terry Christensen)

SOURCE: California Secretary of State.

other parties, and 20.2 percent declared themselves independent (officially known as "decline to state")—see Figure 2.1. The independent percentage has more than doubled since 1986, when it was just 9 percent.

For most of its history, California used **closed primary** elections to select the nominees of each party for state elective office and the U.S. Congress. Voters who are registered with a political party cast their ballots in the primary only for that party's nominees for various offices. The winners of each party's primary election face off in the November general election, when all voters are free to cast their ballots for the candidate of any of the parties. But in 2010, voters approved a "top two" or **open primary** system to go into effect in 2012. In an open primary, no matter what their own party, voters may choose their preferred candidate from any party; the top two vote getters face off in the November election, even if they're from the same party. Advocates of this system hope that instead of concentrating their appeals on the core of their own parties (liberals for Democrats and conservatives for Republicans), candidates will reach out to independent and moderate voters and that those elected will be more moderate and thus more willing to compromise when they get to Sacramento. In theory, this system could break the gridlock in the state capital, but whether it will do so remains to be seen. Meanwhile, the political parties have complained that the open primary system takes away the right of voters registered with their party to choose their own candidates, and it will almost certainly mean that candidates of the minor parties never appear on general election ballots. It's likely that the open primary system will be challenged in court.

Before the Great Depression, California was steadfastly Republican, but during the 1930s a Democratic majority emerged. Since then, the Democrats have dominated in voter registration (see Figure 2.2), although their lead declined from a peak of 60 percent of registered voters in 1942 to a low of 42.7 percent in 2006. Since then, partly due to an exciting presidential election in 2008, Democratic registration has risen slightly—to 44.5 percent in 2010. Meanwhile,

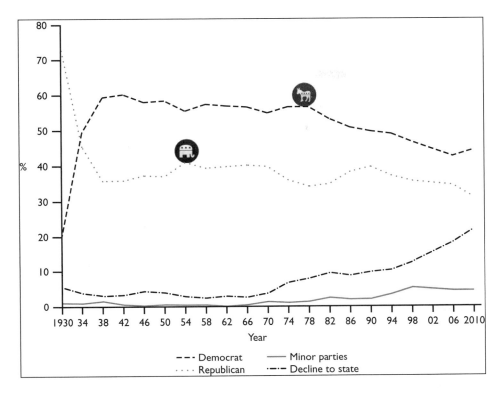

FIGURE 2.2 Party Registration during Gubernatorial Election Years

SOURCE: California Secretary of State

Republican registration has slipped to 30.9 percent. The independent percentage, however, has more than doubled since 1986, when it was just 9 percent. Despite their registration margin, the Democrats did not gain a majority in both houses of the state legislature until 1958. More dramatically, Republican candidates have won eight of the last thirteen gubernatorial elections.

State law dictates party organization, as it does registration and voting. Today's Democratic and Republican parties have similar structures, although the Democrats elect a few more party officials. The state **central committee** is the highest-ranking body in each party. All party candidates and officeholders are automatically members, along with county chairpersons. Officeholders and nominees of each party also appoint members. In addition, Democratic voters elect members from each assembly district, and Republican county central committees elect or appoint members. Each party's state central committee elects a state chair, who functions mainly as the party spokesperson. Although the position traditionally has been powerless, competition for it is sometimes intense.

Beneath the state central committee are county central committees. The voters registered with each party choose committee members every two years in the primary election. The party's nominees for state legislature are also members, as are those who win election. Critics say this system enables officeholders to dominate the grassroots members, but it also ensures that the two levels of party leadership are linked. The state and county party committees play an important role in generating volunteers and contributions for party candidates. They also draft policy positions for party platforms, although candidates and elected officials often ignore these. Despite their low public profile, county committees are sometimes sites of intense conflict among activists. Liberals usually dominate Democratic county central committees, whereas conservatives rule Republican committees. The religious right gained influence in the Republican Party during the 1990s by taking over a majority of the party's county central committees, but since then, moderate Republicans have regained influence in some counties.

California's political parties had an opportunity to strengthen their role in choosing party nominees when the United States Supreme Court overturned the state ban on preprimary endorsements in 1990. California Democrats responded quickly by establishing a preprimary endorsement process that required a candidate to secure at least 60 percent of the delegates at their state convention. The Republican Party declined such endorsements until 2005, when Governor Arnold Schwarzenegger won an early endorsement for reelection and avoided a divisive party primary.

Despite assertions of strengthened party organization, preprimary endorsements don't always matter to California voters. Since the court ruling, Democratic voters have rejected several statewide candidates officially endorsed by their party in primaries, while most party-endorsed candidates who succeeded were incumbents seeking reelection with no opposition in their own party. In 2010, however, the Democratic convention's preprimary endorsement of Assemblyman Dave Jones helped him win the Democratic nomination for state insurance commissioner in an otherwise low-profile race. The influence of such endorsements is limited by the inability of the parties to deliver organizational support to the chosen candidates and by high-spending campaigns and the media, but preprimary endorsements may become more significant when the open primary system goes into effect in 2012.

Party Supporters

Besides the official party organizations, a variety of caucuses and clubs are associated with both major parties. The California Republican Assembly is a staunchly conservative statewide grassroots organization that has dominated the Republican Party, thanks to an activist membership. Republican governor Arnold Schwarzenegger, a moderate, had difficulty with the conservatives in his own party. At the 2007 state party convention, he chastised his fellow California Republicans "for their insularity and narrowness," to which they responded "that they'd rather be ideologically principled than pander to moderates."[1] On the Democratic side, liberals dominate through the California Democratic Council, which comprises hundreds of local Democratic clubs organized by geography, gender, race, ethnicity, or sexual orientation.

Party activists such as these are a tiny percentage of the electorate, however. The remaining support base comes from citizens who designate their party affiliations when they register to vote and usually cast their ballots accordingly. Public opinion polls tell us that voters who prefer the Democratic Party tend to be sympathetic to the poor and immigrants; concerned about health care, education, and the environment; in favor of gay rights, gun control, and abortion rights; and supportive of tax increases to provide public services. Those who prefer the Republican Party are more likely to oppose these views and to worry more about big government and high taxes. Of course, many people mix these positions.[2]

Both major parties enjoy widespread support, but the more liberal Democratic Party fares better with blacks; city dwellers; union members; and residents of Los Angeles, Sacramento, and the San Francisco Bay Area (see Figure 2.3). Latino voters also favor Democrats, a tendency that was strengthened by Republican support for several statewide initiatives relating to immigration and affirmative action. Voters among most Asian nationalities identify themselves as Democratic, but some (notably Chinese and Vietnamese) lean Republican. Voters with ties to China, India, and Vietnam are also more likely to register as independents than are other Californians. As with Latinos, Asian loyalties to the California Republican Party were weakened by its sponsorship of initiatives perceived as anti-immigrant in the 1990s. Thanks in large part to the failure of Republicans to win support from minority voters, Democrats currently enjoy majorities in the state legislature and congressional delegation, and California is considered a solidly "blue" (Democratic) state—despite occasional Republican victories for statewide offices.

The more conservative Republican Party does better with whites, suburbanites, rural voters, and in Orange County, the Central Valley, and inland California, as well as with older, more affluent voters and with Christian conservatives. These constituencies are more likely to turn out to vote than those that support Democrats, which is why Republicans sometimes win statewide elections despite their registration disadvantage.

In the past, Republican candidates were also successful because they could often win the support of Democratic voters thanks to cross-filing (until 1958), charismatic candidates, clever campaigns, and split-ticket voting. But in the 1990s, ticket splitting declined, and instead, voters increasingly voted a straight party-line ticket—either all Democratic or all Republican.[3] This includes decline-to-state voters, who, contrary to common wisdom, are not necessarily "independent": 42 percent lean Democratic, and 28 percent lean Republican.[4] Some observers assert that the rightward thrust of the Republican Party drove independent voters to the Democrats and was even more important to the Democratic Party's continued success than was winning over minority voters.[5] Republicans who can present themselves as moderates, as did gubernatorial candidates Arnold Schwarzenegger in 2003 and Meg Whitman in 2010, may have proved this thesis by winning the votes of many independents and some Democrats, thus demonstrating that Californians will still indulge in split-ticket voting, at least on occasion.

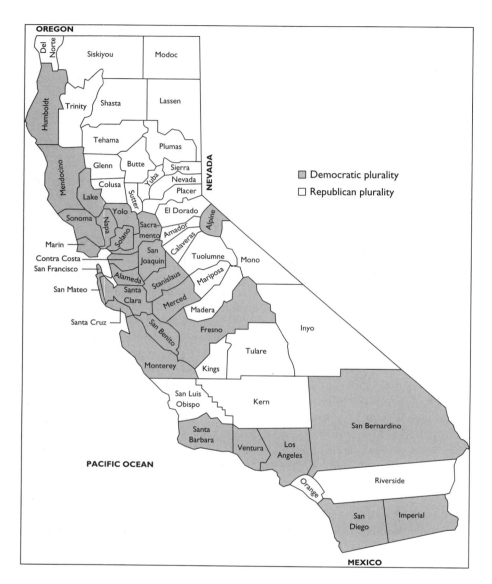

FIGURE 2.3 California's Partisan Division by County, 2010. (Courtesy of Terry Christensen)

SOURCE: California Secretary of State

DIRECT DEMOCRACY

Party politics is only one way Californians participate in the political process. To counter the railroad machine's control of state and local government, the Progressive reformers also guaranteed the people a say through the mechanisms of direct democracy introduced in Chapter 1: the recall, the referendum, and the initiative. Referenda and initiatives appear on our ballots as "propositions," with numbers assigned by the secretary of state; local measures are assigned letters by the county clerk.

The Recall

The least-used form of direct democracy is the **recall**, by which the voters can remove officeholders at all levels of government between scheduled elections. Advocates circulate a recall petition with a statement of their reasons for wanting the official in question to be removed from office. They must collect a specific number of voter signatures within a specific period. The numbers vary with the office in question. At the local level, for example, the number of signatures required to qualify a recall for the ballot varies between 10 and 30 percent of those who voted in the previous local election; these signatures must be collected over periods that vary between 40 and 160 days. A recall petition for a judge or a legislator requires signatures equaling 20 percent of the vote in the last state election, while for state executive officeholders, the figure is 12 percent. In all these cases, petitioners have 160 days to collect the signatures. If enough signatures are collected by advocates and validated by the secretary of state (for a state officeholder) or by the county clerk (for a local officeholder), an election is held. The ballot is simple: "Shall [name] be removed from the office of [title]?" The recall takes effect if a majority of voters vote yes, and then either an election or an appointment—whichever state or local law requires—fills the vacancy for the office. Elected officials who are recalled cannot be candidates in the replacement election.

Recalling state officeholders is easier in California than in the other seventeen states where recall is possible. All but one of these states require more signatures, and while any reason suffices in California, most other states require corruption or malfeasance by the officeholder. Nevertheless, recalls are rare in California, where the process has been used most extensively and successfully in local government, particularly by parents who are angry with school board members. Even so, only a dozen or so recalls are on local ballots in any given year, and only about half of the officials who face recall are removed from office. Two of California's state senators were recalled in 1913, but no other state officeholders were removed until 1995, when two legislators were recalled during a struggle between Democrats and Republicans over control of the state assembly.

Then, spectacularly, Governor Gray Davis was recalled in 2003. Davis had narrowly won reelection in November 2002; three months later, opponents launched their recall petition. Thirty-one previous attempts to recall a California governor had failed to make the ballot, and most political observers assumed that the petitioners would fail to acquire the 897,158 valid signatures required to qualify for an election. But they underestimated voter discontent, not only with Davis but also with the general condition of California politics. Despite his reelection, Davis's approval rating in public opinion polls had sunk to just 24 percent when signature gathering began.[6] His decline in popularity was a result of his cautious leadership during the state's energy crisis in 2001, a recession, a huge budget deficit, and the inability of the legislature and the governor to agree on solutions to these problems. Davis's aloof personality also contributed to his problems. His recall opponents discovered a groundswell of support, facilitated by conservative talk radio hosts and the availability of the Internet to circulate petitions. Even so, signature gathering was slow until Republican congressman Darrell Issa contributed $2 million to pay for professionals to assist.

In July 2003, the secretary of state certified that 1.3 million valid signatures had been gathered—far more than required—and the election was set for October. Ultimately, 135 candidates qualified to run, including actor Arnold Schwarzenegger. His seventy-five-day campaign took the state by storm, gaining far more media and public attention than any regular election in recent memory—thanks in part to his status as a movie star. On Election Day, 55.4 percent of the voters said yes to recall, and Schwarzenegger easily outpaced all other replacement candidates with 48.6 percent of the vote. For the first time in California history—and only the second time ever in the United States—a governor had been recalled.

The Referendum

The **referendum** is another form of direct democracy. A referendum allows the voters to nullify acts of the legislature. Referendum advocates have ninety days after the legislature makes a law to collect a number of signatures equal to 5 percent of the votes cast for governor in the previous election (510,756 based on the 2010 vote). Referenda are even rarer than recalls. Of the forty-seven referenda on California ballots since 1912, voters have rejected acts of the legislature twenty-eight times. In 2004, business groups qualified a referendum on health-care legislation approved in Governor Davis's last days in office. The hard-fought campaign pitted liberals, unions, and Democrats who supported the program against conservatives, business leaders, and Republicans. In the end, the voters narrowly rejected the health-care legislation, even though nearly 20 percent of Californians lacked health insurance. In 2008, competing gambling interests challenged the state's tribal gaming agreements in referenda, but the voters approved the agreements.

The Initiative

Recalls and referenda are reactions to what elected officials do; in contrast, the **initiative** allows citizens to make policy themselves by drafting a new law or a constitutional amendment and then circulating petitions to get it onto the ballot. Qualifying a proposed law requires a number of signatures equal to 5 percent of the votes cast for governor in the last election; constitutional amendments require a number of signatures equal to 8 percent (817,215 based on California's 2010 election). If enough valid signatures are obtained within 150 days, the initiative goes to the voters at the next election or, on rare occasions, in a special election called by the governor.

The subjects of initiatives vary wildly and are often controversial. In the past, voters have approved limits on bilingual education, banned the slaughter of horses for human consumption, and defined marriage as a relationship between a man and a woman only. Other recent propositions have dealt with tribal gambling

T A B L E 2.1 **The Track Record of State Initiatives**

Time Period	Number	Number Adopted	Number Rejected
1912–1919	31	8	23
1920–1929	34	10	24
1930–1939	37	10	27
1940–1949	20	7	13
1950–1959	11	1	10
1960–1969	10	3	7
1970–1979	24	7	17
1980–1989	52	25	27
1990–1999	50	20	30
2000–2009	65	20	45
2010	11	4	7
Total	345	115 (33.3%)	230 (66.7%)

SOURCE: California Secretary of State.

(repeatedly), redistricting (repeatedly), stem cell research, DNA sampling, and mental health services. In 2010 voters considered legalization of marijuana, redistricting (again), suspension of air-pollution control laws, funding of local governments, and a vehicle license fee to support state parks—and more.

Twenty-three other states provide for the initiative, but few rely on it as heavily as California. Initiatives were common between 1912 and 1939, but declined in number during the next four decades (see Table 2.1). Then **political consultants**, interest groups, and governors rediscovered the initiative, and ballot measures proliferated. The 1988 and 1990 election year ballots witnessed an explosion, with eighteen initiatives on each. In 2010 voters faced a total of fourteen propositions in the primary and general elections, including both citizen-generated and legislative initiatives.

Legislative Initiatives, Constitutional Amendments, and Bonds

Propositions can also be placed on the ballot by the state legislature. Such **legislative initiatives** can include new laws that the legislature prefers to put before the voters rather than enact on its own, or proposed **constitutional amendments**, for which voter approval is compulsory. The 2010 open primary measure, for example, was put on the ballot by the legislature as part of a deal to win the vote of a Republican senator for the proposed budget.

Voter approval is also required when the governor or the legislature seeks to issue **bonds** (borrowing money) to finance parks, schools, transportation, or other capital-intensive projects. Few of these proposals are controversial, and more than 60 percent pass with minimal campaigning or spending. In the 2006 and 2008 elections, voters approved $29 billion in bonds for projects ranging from high-speed trains to aid for veterans.

THE POLITICS OF BALLOT PROPOSITIONS

The proliferation of ballot propositions is hardly the result of a sudden surge in democratic participation. Rather, it stems largely from the opportunism of special interests, individual politicians, and public relations firms. One man, hoping for cures to diseases suffered by his mother and son, provided the $3 million that funded the initiative to support stem cell research in 2004. Hundreds of millions of dollars have been spent on ballot measures regulating casinos on Native American lands, the most recent of which appeared on the ballot in 2008. In 2010, Pacific Gas and Electric and Mercury Insurance single-handedly funded separate initiatives that were clearly in their self-interest, and both the Chamber of Commerce and the Democratic Party funded measures affecting their own pet causes.

Although intended as mechanisms for citizens to shape policy, even the most grassroots-driven initiatives cost half a million dollars to qualify and millions more to mount a successful campaign. "If you pay enough," declared Ronald George, then chief justice of the California Supreme Court, "you can get anything on the ballot. You pay a little bit more and you get it passed."[7] In 2006 the pro and con campaigns on a proposition that would have imposed a modest fee on oil extraction spent $152 million, with oil companies spending $93 million on the measure. The campaigns for and against the 2008 proposition banning same-sex marriage spent a total of $83 million—much of it coming from out of state, because California is often seen as setting precedents for campaigns elsewhere. Total spending for proposition campaigns in any given election year now averages nearly $300 million. Much of it comes from corporations and unions. According to the California Fair Political Practices Commission, "These interests have spent hundreds of millions of dollars for and against ballot measures. They often win by spending money to defeat measures, which has the effect of maintaining the status quo.... . The conclusion is inescapable: A handful of special interests have a disproportionate amount of influence on California elections and public policy."[8]

Besides wealthy individuals such as international financier George Soros (a supporter of drug decriminalization) and high-tech executive Tim Draper (a supporter of school vouchers), politicians have also discovered initiatives as a way to further their own careers or shape public policy. Republican governor Pete Wilson helped secure reelection in 1994 by sponsoring a successful measure on illegal immigration. In 2002 then movie star Arnold Schwarzenegger sponsored an initiative to fund after-school programs, advancing both that cause and his political career. As governor, Schwarzenegger tried to use ballot measures to further his agenda when thwarted by the Democratic majority in the legislature. In a succession of elections, he put forward initiatives addressing political and budget reforms, as well as bond measures. The bond measures passed, but most of the reforms were rejected by the voters, much to the disappointment of the governor.

Others also take advantage of direct democracy. Public relations firms and **political consultants**, virtual "guns for hire," have developed lucrative careers managing initiative and referenda campaigns; they offer expertise in public opinion polling, computer-targeted mailing, and television advertising—the staples of modern campaigns. Some firms generate initiatives themselves by conducting test mailings and preliminary polls in hopes of snagging big contracts from proposition sponsors. With millions of dollars in campaign spending hanging in the balance, big economic interests gain an advantage over grassroots efforts—surely not what the Progressives intended.

Nevertheless, direct democracy offers hope to the relatively powerless by enabling them to take their case to the public. In 2004 voters showed sympathy for those with little power when they approved Proposition 63, which increased taxes on the rich to fund mental health programs. In 2008, a proposition on the treatment of farm animals passed, despite the strong opposition of agribusiness. In 2010, environmentalists got a measure to fund state parks on the ballot and local governments qualified an initiative restricting state's ability to "take back" local funds at will (see Chapter 9). The former proposition was soundly defeated, but the latter passed easily. Almost every California ballot includes initiatives generated by grassroots groups. Although these initiatives are often defeated by well-funded corporate interests, at least direct democracy provides such groups an opportunity to make their cases.

Unfortunately, direct democracy does not necessarily result in good laws. Because self-interested sponsors draft initiatives and media masters run campaigns, careful and rational deliberation is rare. Flaws or contradictions in successful initiatives may take years to resolve. Sometimes this is done through the implementation of the measures by government agencies or through the legislative process. Increasingly, however, disputes about initiatives are resolved in state and federal courts, which must rule on whether the initiatives are consistent with other laws and with the state and federal constitutions. In recent years, courts have overturned all or parts of initiatives dealing with illegal immigration, campaign finance, and same-sex marriage, for example (see Chapter 6). Although such rulings seem to deny the will of the voters, the electorate cannot make laws that contradict the state or federal constitutions.

The increased use of direct democracy has also had an impact on the power of our elected representatives. Although we expect them to make policy, their ability to do so has been constrained by a sequence of initiatives in recent decades. This is particularly the case with the state budget, much of which is dictated by past ballot measures rather than the legislature or the governor.

The proliferation of initiatives, expensive and deceptive campaigns, flawed laws, and court interventions have annoyed voters and policymakers alike. Perhaps as a consequence, two-thirds of all initiatives are rejected (see Table 2–1). Although Californians express anger and frustration with the initiative process, a solid majority of survey respondents support direct democracy in concept. At the same time, a majority favors reforms such as a review of ballot language and legal issues before initiatives are placed on the ballot.[9]

POLITICAL PARTIES AND DIRECT DEMOCRACY

Authors Mark Baldassare and Cheryl Katz argue that California has evolved into a unique "hybrid democracy," with power divided between elected representatives and the public.[10] Partisan gridlock in Sacramento, voter distrust, and powerful interest groups (see Chapter 4) have resulted in the increased reliance on direct democracy to resolve issues, albeit often imperfectly. California's political parties can't break the gridlock or even control the choice of their own candidates in an electoral system in which money seems to trump party organization. Once elected, our officials seem unable to resolve the issues that confront us. Direct democracy provides an alternative—for political leaders, moneyed interests, and citizens—yet the proliferation of propositions further confounds voters. Does California have too much democracy? Sometimes it seems so. Some voters feel overwhelmed and turned off, but most manage to sift through complex initiatives and seductive campaigns to find the candidates and policies that suit their preferences.

NOTES

1. Peter Schrag, "On Race and Gender, the GOP's Tent Is Teeny," *Sacramento Bee,* September 19, 2007.

2. See Public Policy Institute of California, "California Voter and Party Profiles," *Just the Facts,* September 2009, www.ppic.org (accessed June 24, 2010); and past reports of the PPIC Statewide Survey, also at www.ppic.org.

3. See Gary C. Jacobson, "Partisanship and Ideological Polarization in the California Electorate," *State Politics and Policy Quarterly* 4 (2004): 113–139.

4. Public Policy Institute of California, "California's Likely Voters," *Just the Facts,* September 2009, www.ppic.org (accessed June 24, 2010).

5. Morris P. Fiorina and Samuel J. Abrams, "Is California Really a Blue State?" in *The New Political Geography of California,* ed. Frederick Douzet, Thad Kousser, and Kenneth P. Miller (Berkeley: Berkeley Public Policy Press, Institute of Governmental Studies, University of California, 2008).

6. "State of the Golden State," Public Policy Institute of California, San Francisco: Public Policy Institute of California, August 2003, www.ppic.org.

7. Ronald George, "Promoting Judicial Independence," *The Commonwealth,* February 2006, p. 9.

8. California Fair Political Practices Commission, *Big Money Talks,* March 2010, p. 6, www.fppc.ca.gov/reports/Report38104.pdf (accessed June 25, 2010).

9.   Public Policy Institute of California, "Californians and Their Government," Statewide Survey, December 2008, www.ppic.org (accessed June 25, 2010).

10. Mark Baldassare and Cheryl Katz, *The Coming Age of Direct Democracy* (New York: Rowman & Littlefield, 2008).

LEARN MORE ON THE WEB

Polling data, including archives:
  www.field.com/fieldpoll or www.ppic.org

California's political parties:
  American Independent Party: www.aipca.org
  California Democratic Party: www.cadem.org
  California Republican Party: www.cagop.org
  Green Party of California: www.cagreens.org
  Libertarian Party of California: www.ca.lp.org
  Peace and Freedom Party: www.peaceandfreedom.org

Information on electoral reform:
  www.cgs.org

Information on ballot propositions:
  www.calvoter.org or www.ss.ca.gov

LEARN MORE AT THE LIBRARY

John Allswang. *The Initiative and Referendum in California, 1897–1998.* Stanford, Calif.: Stanford University Press, 2000.

Mark Baldassare and Cheryl Katz. *The Coming Age of Direct Democracy.* New York: Rowman & Littlefield, 2008.

Center for Government Studies. *Democracy by Initiative.* 2d ed. 2008. www.cgs.org (accessed June 24, 2010).

Larry N. Gerston and Terry Christensen, *Recall! California's Political Earthquake.* Armonk, N.Y.: M. E. Sharpe, 2004.

3

California Elections, Campaigns, and the Media

CHAPTER CONTENTS

A typical California ballot requires voters to make decisions about more than twenty elective positions and propositions. Even the best-informed citizens sometimes find it difficult to choose among candidates for offices they know little about and to decide on obscure and complicated propositions. Political party labels provide some guidance, but candidates, campaigns, and the media are also crucial in the California elections.

Campaigns and the media are especially important because of the mobility and rootlessness that characterize California society. More than half of all Californians were born elsewhere, and many voters in every California state election are participating for the first time. Residents also move frequently within the state, reducing the political influence of families, friends, and peer groups and boosting that of campaigns and the media.

THE VOTERS

California citizens who are eighteen years or older are eligible to vote unless they are in prison or a mental institution. Those eligible must **register to vote**, which must be done at least fifteen days before an election by completing a form available at post offices, fire stations, libraries, and public places where party activists eagerly solicit new voters. Registration forms are also available with applications for driver's licenses and at social service agencies or online at www.sos.ca.gov/nvrc/dedform. Once registered, those who cast their ballots regularly stay on the voter rolls indefinitely. Occasionally, however, voter lists are "purged" of voters who have not participated for some time or who have died or moved.

Altogether, nearly 23.4 million Californians are eligible to vote. Only 17 million (72.4 percent) were registered in 2010, however, and as few as 8 million actually vote in some elections—somewhat below the national average. In the gubernatorial election of 2010, turnout among those registered to vote was 59 percent. Turnout is higher in presidential elections. In 2008, 79.4 percent of the state's registered voters participated, a rate that was higher than the national average. In the 2010 primary election, however, only 33.3 percent of those registered actually participated—a record low for a gubernatorial primary election.

Traditionally, voters go to designated polling places to cast their ballots, but today nearly half **vote by mail**, having requested absentee ballots from their county registrar of voters. Those who prefer to cast their ballots this way can sign up as "permanent" absentee voters so that ballots are automatically sent to them for every election. In the 2010 gubernatorial primary election, a record 58 percent of those who voted did so by absentee ballot. Most of these people simply prefer the convenience of voting by mail given their busy lives; many prefer to deal with the complex ballots at their leisure; and still others vote absentee because campaigns push identified supporters to vote by mail to ensure their participation. With so many more people voting absentee—up to three weeks before Election Day—campaigns have had to change their tactics. Rather than a big push in the last few days, they must spread their resources and extend their messages over a longer period.

Voting by mail may have increased participation slightly, but even with this convenience, many Californians choose not to vote. Some don't get around to registering. Millions more who are registered still don't vote. Some are apathetic, some are unaware, and others feel too uninformed to act. Still others believe that voting is a charade because politics "is controlled by special interests." Some people say election information is "too hard to understand," and others are bewildered by all the messages that bombard them during a typical California election. But the reason that people most frequently give for not voting is that they are too busy.[1]

Yet political campaigns are designed to motivate voters to support candidates and causes. This task is complicated, though, because those who vote are not a representative cross section of the actual population. Non-Latino whites, for example, make up 42 percent of the population but 65 percent of the electorate.

Although Latinos, African Americans, and Asians constitute 58 percent of California's population, they are only 35 percent of the voters in primary and general elections.[2] This disparity in turnout means that California's voting electorate is not representative of the state's population. The lower participation rate among Latinos and Asians is partly explained by the relative youth of these populations (about one-third of Latinos, for example, are too young to vote) and by the fact that many are not yet citizens.

Language, culture, and socioeconomic status may also be barriers to registration and voting among minority groups. This situation is changing, however; Latinos were just 8 percent of the state's registered voters in 1978 but are more than 21 percent today,[3] and the number continues to rise. Still, voter registration lags among Latino citizens, with only about half of those eligible currently registered to vote.[4]

Differences in the levels of voter participation do not end with ethnicity. The people most likely to vote are suburban homeowners and Republicans, who tend to be richer, better educated, and older. Lower levels of participation are usually found among poorer, less educated, and younger inner-city residents and Democrats.[5] According to recent reports, 78 percent of adults over the age of sixty-five are "likely voters," while just 24 percent of adults aged eighteen to

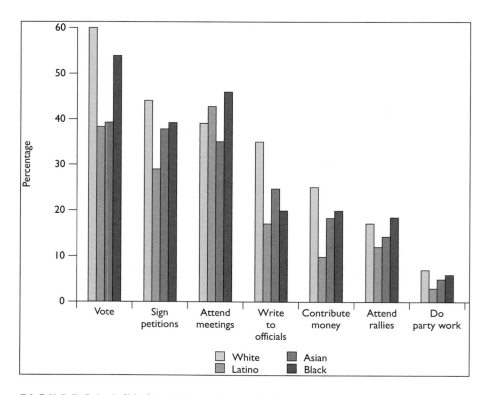

FIGURE 3.1 Political Participation by Ethnic Groups

SOURCE: From Public Policy Institute of California, "The Ties That Bind," 2004. Reprinted with permission.

twenty-four are "likely to participate in elections."[6] All this adds up to a voting electorate that is more conservative than the population as a whole, which explains how Republicans sometimes win statewide elections despite the Democratic edge in registration and why liberal ballot measures rarely pass.

Of course, voting is only one form of political participation. Many people sign petitions, attend public meetings, write letters or e-mails to officials, and contribute money to campaigns. But as we see in Figure 3.1, the number participating diminishes with each form of engagement, and differences among ethnic groups persist. As with voting, those who participate most are white, older, more affluent, homeowners, and more highly educated. Does the differential in voting and other forms of participation matter? It seems self-evident that elected officials pay more attention to the concerns of those who participate than those who do not.

THE CANDIDATES

When we vote, we choose among candidates, but where do candidates come from? Some are encouraged to run by political parties or interest groups seeking to advance their causes. Political leaders looking for allies recruit others, although weak political parties make such overtures less common in California than elsewhere. Most California candidates are self-starters with an interest in politics who decide to run and then seek support. The rising cost and increasing negativity of campaigns have discouraged some people from running, although wealthy individuals who can fund their own campaigns have frequently appeared as candidates in recent years. Most candidates start at the bottom of the political ladder, running for school board or city council, and work their way up, building support as they go. Others gain experience as staff members for elected officials, eventually running for their boss's job. Wealthy candidates sometimes skip such apprenticeships and run directly for higher office, but the voters are sometimes skeptical about their lack of political experience.

Historically, candidates in California have been even less representative of the population than the electorate. Most have been educated white males of above-average financial means. The 1990s brought change, however. Underrepresented groups such as women, racial and ethnic minorities, and gay men and lesbians grew in strength and organization, and structural changes facilitated their candidacies. A 1990 initiative limited the number of terms that legislators could serve, thus ensuring greater turnover in the state legislature. In addition, the redistricting decisions after the censuses of 1990 and 2000 resulted in redrawn legislative and congressional districts that gave minority candidates new opportunities at both levels. This could happen again with the redistricting that will follow the 2010 census, when district boundaries will be revised by a citizens' commission created by initiative rather than by the legislators themselves.

Latinos have gained the most from these changes, obtaining a sizable delegation in the state legislature and the California congressional delegation. Latinos have also gained representation at the local level, electing more than 1,200 of California's county supervisors, city council members, mayors, and school board members.[7] Most Latino officeholders are Democrats.

Although a smaller minority, African Americans gained a foothold in state politics earlier, including the statewide positions of lieutenant governor and superintendent of public instruction. Three African Americans have served as speaker of the assembly (its most powerful leader), but overall, black representation has shrunk as that of other minorities has increased.

Asian Americans remain the most underrepresented of California's racial minorities. In the past, Asian Americans have won election to statewide offices, including U.S. senator, secretary of state, and state treasurer. John Chiang, a Democrat of Chinese descent, was elected state controller in 2006 and re-elected in 2010. Electing candidates has been difficult for Asian Americans, however, because many are recent immigrants who are not yet rooted in the state's political system and because of cultural and political differences among the Chinese, Japanese, Vietnamese, Filipinos, Koreans, Indo-Americans, and others. But these groups have generated more candidates in every recent election. Many [Asians] have won local offices on city councils and school boards, and nine serve in the state legislature.

Women candidates have been more successful. Both of California's U.S. senators are now women. Women have been elected to statewide office in the past, although only one, Secretary of State Deborah Bowen, is currently serving. A substantial number of women are in the state legislature, however, including Assembly Majority Leader Fiona Ma. Many of California's city council members, mayors, and county supervisors also are women.

Lesbians and gay men achieved elected office later than any of these groups. Greater bias may be a factor, and in the past, the closeted status of many homosexuals—including candidates and elected officials—weakened organizing efforts and made gay and lesbian elective successes invisible. Nevertheless, eighty openly gay and lesbian individuals have won election to local offices (including sixteen judges),[8] and seven serve in the state legislature. Some, such as Assembly Speaker John Perez a Democrat from Los Angeles, have risen to leadership positions.

Racism and sexism partly explain the underrepresentation of all these groups, but other factors contribute as well. Many members of these groups are economically disadvantaged, which makes it hard to participate in politics, let alone to take on the demands of a candidacy. Women, minorities, and gay men and lesbians are usually not plugged in to the network of lobbyists, interest groups, and big donors that provide funds for California's expensive campaigns. Minorities also have difficulty winning support outside their own groups and may alienate their natural constituencies in the process. The fact that minorities are less likely to vote than Anglos further reduces their candidates' potential. Nevertheless, organizations within each of these constituencies work to recruit, train, and support candidates, and the diversity of California candidates and elected officials increases with each election.

THE MONEY

The introduction of primary elections in 1909 shifted the focus of campaigns from political parties to individual candidates. Political aspirants must raise money, recruit workers, research issues, and plot strategy on their own or with the help of expensive consultants rather than with that of political parties, which contribute little in the way of money or staff. California campaigns thus tend to focus on the personalities of the candidates more than on parties or policies.

Weak parties mean that candidates must promote themselves, so the cost of running for state assembly or senate often exceeds $1 million. Spending on races for the legislature totaled $97.7 million in the 2007–2008 election cycle.[9] Campaigns for statewide offices are even more expensive. The top two candidates for governor spent over $210 million in 2010.

Interest groups, businesses, and wealthy individuals provide the money. Much campaign financing is provided by **political action committees (PACs)**, which interest groups use to direct money to preferred campaigns. Legislative leaders such as the speaker of the assembly and the president pro tem of the senate raise huge sums from such sources and channel the money to their allies in the legislature; individual candidates raise money by asking potential contributors for donations directly and by organizing special fund-raising events, which range from coffees and barbecues to banquets and concerts. They also solicit contributions from specific audiences through targeted mailings and the Internet.

Increasingly, however, it appears that candidates must be wealthy enough to finance their own campaigns. Arnold Schwarzenegger provided more than $10 million for his campaigns in 2003 and 2006, but Republican Meg Whitman broke state and national records by spending $71 million of her own money to win the Republican nomination for governor in 2010 and then spending another $71 million in the general election. Voters are skeptical about wealthy candidates who self-finance their campaigns, however, and in the past, most such candidates have lost.

Worried about the influence of money and turned off by campaign advertising, Californians have approved a series of initiatives aimed at regulating campaign finance. The **Political Reform Act of 1974** required public disclosure of all donors and expenditures through the **Fair Political Practices Commission (FPPC)**. Since then, reformers have tried repeatedly to limit the amount that individuals and groups can contribute, but several initiatives approved by the voters were invalidated by the courts on grounds that they limited free speech. In 2000 voters approved Proposition 34, a legislative initiative setting higher contribution limits for individuals and committees (see Table 3.1).

Proposition 34 also set voluntary spending limits for candidates (see Table 3.2). Those who accept the limits have their photo and candidate statements published in the official ballot booklets that go to all voters; candidates who decline the limits are excluded from the booklet. Most candidates for the legislature and statewide offices other than governor comply with the spending limits; those who don't lose the moral high ground to those who do, which may influence voters. There is no limit,

T A B L E   3.1   Proposition 34 Limits on Contributions to State Candidates, 2009–2010

Contributor	Legislature	Statewide except Governor	Governor
Person	$3,900	$ 6,500	$25,000
Small contributor committee	$7,800	$12,900	$25,900
Political party	No limit	No limit	No limit

SOURCE: California Fair Political Practices Commission, www.fppc.ca.gov.

T A B L E   3.2   Voluntary Expenditure Ceilings for Candidates for State Offices, 2009–2010

Office	Primary	General Election
Assembly	$518,000	$906,000
Senate	777,000	1,165,000
Governor	7,768,000	12,946,000
Other statewide offices	5,178,000	7,768,000

SOURCE: California Fair Political Practices Commission, www.fppc.ca.gov.

however, on how much a candidate can contribute to his or her own campaign, which enables candidates such as Whitman to substantially fund their campaigns.

Like most reforms, Proposition 34 has had unintended consequences. Money is given to political parties to spend on behalf of candidates rather than to the candidates themselves, which may ultimately increase the power of the parties—and such contributions jumped dramatically after Proposition 34. More significantly, the new spending limits have been subverted by **independent expenditures** by PACs or groups specially organized by political consultants in support of candidates. Since Proposition 34, over $110 million has been spent in this way, including $32 million for the gubernatorial candidates in 2010. Jerry Brown, the victor, was the primary beneficiary.[10] Top independent expenditure groups include the prison guards' union, Indian gaming interests, and the California Teachers Association.[11] In some campaigns, independent expenditures exceed those of the candidates. The only restriction on independent expenditures is that they cannot be coordinated with the campaigns of the candidates they support. Because they are not directly associated with the candidates, "independent" mailings and television ads often feature the most vicious attacks on opponents.

Between various loopholes in Proposition 34, independent expenditures, PACs with names that cloak their real purpose and backers, and PACs that contribute to other PACs to obscure the individuals and interests who contribute the money, the Proposition 34 regulations have been condemned as "ineffective hypocrisy,"[12] even as reformers seek ways to close the loopholes. Twenty-five other states limit the impact of money on politics by providing some form of public financing for campaigns, but Californians rejected initiatives proposing such a system in the 2006 and 2010 elections.

CAMPAIGNING CALIFORNIA STYLE

Campaign contributors hope to elect allies who will support their interests. They also expect their money to buy immediate access and long-term influence. Candidates deny making specific deals, however, insisting that they and their contributors merely share views on key issues. Millions of dollars flow into candidates' coffers through this murky relationship. In the 2010 election, for example, labor unions generously supported Democrat Jerry Brown, while business interests gave to Meg Whitman. Some donors give to candidates of both parties, just to cover their bases.

So much money is needed because California campaigns, whether local or statewide, are highly professionalized. To supplement political party support, candidates hire political consultants and management firms to perform a variety of functions, including recruiting workers, raising money, advertising, conducting public opinion polls, and performing virtually all other campaign activities. These specialists understand the workings of California's volatile electorate and use their knowledge to a candidate's benefit. California's top-ranked political consultants include Gale Kaufman and Garry South, who work for Democratic candidates, and Frank Schubert, who works for Republicans.[13]

Television has made campaign management firms indispensable, allowing candidates instant entry into voters' homes. It also enables candidates to put their message across at the exact moment of their choosing—on broadcast or cable TV, between wrestling bouts, during the local news or *Oprah,* or just after *American Idol,* depending on the targeted audience. The efficacy of the medium is proved repeatedly when relatively unknown candidates spend big money on television commercials and become major contenders, as eBay billionaire Meg Whitman did when she saturated the airwaves beginning in late 2009 in the 2010 race for governor. A statewide advertising buy on television costs at least $1 million—and one round of ads is never enough. Although initially a leader in the Republican race for the U.S. Senate nomination in 2010, former congressman Tom Campbell was effectively eliminated when he lacked funds to compete on television.

More than in smaller, more compact states where people are more connected, Californians rely heavily on television for political information. As a consequence, television advertising accounts for as much as 80 percent of all spending for statewide races in California. In such a big state, it is the only way to reach the mass of voters. At the height of the gubernatorial campaigns, candidates run hundreds of ads a day in California's major media markets. Well-funded initiative campaigns also rely almost exclusively on television advertising.

Television is too costly for most candidates for legislative and local offices, however. A thirty-second prime-time spot can cost more than $20,000 in Los Angeles, and because most television stations broadcast to audiences much larger than a legislative district, the message is wasted on many viewers. Advertising during the day or on cable is cheaper, however, and many legislative candidates have turned to these alternatives. Most, however, have found a more efficient way to spend their money: **direct mail**. Computers have revolutionized political mail by enabling campaign strategists to target selected voters with personal messages.

Direct-mail experts develop lists of voters and their characteristics and then send special mailings to people who share particular qualities. In addition to listing voters by party registration and residence, these experts compile data banks that identify various groups, including liberals and conservatives, ethnic voters, retired people, homeowners and renters, union members, women, gay men and lesbians, and those most likely to vote. Campaigns even do data mining on consumer interests that might predict the political or policy concerns of voters so their mailing can be microtargeted. Once the targets have been identified, campaign strategists can develop just the right message to send to them. Conservatives may be told of the candidate's opposition to gay marriage; liberals may be promised action on the environment. For the price of a single thirty-second television spot, local or legislative candidates can send multiple mailings to their selected audiences.

Television and direct mail dominate California campaigns because they reach the most voters, but the use of these media is not without problems. Because television and direct mail are expensive, campaign costs have risen, as has the influence of major donors. Candidates who are unable to raise vast sums of money are usually left at the starting gate. Incumbent officeholders, who are masters at fund-raising and are well connected to major contributors, become invincible. Furthermore, these media are criticized for oversimplifying issues and emphasizing the negative. Television commercials for ballot measures reduce complicated issues to emotional thirty-second spots aimed at uninformed voters. Candidates' ads and mailings indulge in the same oversimplification, often in the form of attacks on opponents. When the candidates portray each other negatively, voters may feel that they must choose the lesser evil rather than make a decision on the policies and positive traits of the candidates. Voters have grown skeptical of such attacks, yet they are hard to resist. Campaign consultants, who are usually blamed for the phenomenon, point out that campaigns had a nasty edge even a century ago and that the public pays more attention to negative messages than to positive ones.

Candidates also take their campaigns to the Internet, with Web sites and e-mail lists to communicate with the media and with supporters. Former eBay executive Meg Whitman, perhaps not surprisingly given her background, spent nearly $3 million on website development and information technology during the 2010 gubernatorial primary, building what was described as the "Cadillac" Web site.[14] The political impact of Internet campaigning is unclear, however.

Whereas television and mail enable candidates to reach us whether we're interested or not, voters must initiate contact on the Internet, which limits the audience to those who are already engaged. Interest groups, however, can use e-mail to send campaign messages to their members, and some candidates have targeted e-mails to particular constituencies, such as Christian conservatives. The Internet can also help candidates recruit volunteers and solicit donations.

Overall, California's media-oriented campaigns reinforce both the emphasis on candidates' personalities and voter cynicism. Some people blame such campaigns for declining voter turnout. Contemporary campaigns may also depress voter turnout by aiming all their efforts at regular voters and ignoring those who are less likely to vote—often minority voters. Although this is a sensible way to use campaign resources, it is not a way to stimulate democracy.

Some candidates try to revive old-fashioned door-to-door or telephone campaigns and get-out-the-vote drives on Election Day. Labor union volunteers have become a force in elections in Los Angeles and San Jose, for example, and the Democratic and Republican parties rely on volunteers to turn out voters for their candidates. Grassroots campaigns have a long and honorable tradition in California, but even in small-scale, local races, they are often up against not only big-money opponents but also the California lifestyle: few people are at home to be contacted, and those who are may let calls go to voice mail or be mistrustful of strangers at their door. For good or ill, candidates need money for their campaigns; those with the most money don't always win, but those with too little rarely even become contenders.

Many of the traditional means of contacting voters were tossed out in the recall election of 2003, when the brevity of the campaign and the candidacy of Arnold Schwarzenegger changed everything. State law required a single election, rather than a primary and a general election, to be held within sixty to eighty days of the certification of the recall petition. Normally, statewide elections sprawl over at least a year, but when the election was set for October 7, Governor Davis and the candidates to replace him had just seventy-five days to make their cases, resulting in the most intense campaign in California history. Candidates who were well known or who could raise funds quickly, such as Democratic lieutenant governor Cruz Bustamante and Republican Arnold Schwarzenegger, had an immediate head start. But Schwarzenegger had another advantage. As an internationally famous and glamorous movie star, he attracted massive—and free—coverage by the news media within California and beyond.

Although media coverage of the brief campaign was different, some elements of the recall were not. The major candidates relied on television ads and mailings more than ever because time was too short to organize more traditional outreach efforts. Even in so short a campaign, more than $85 million was spent. Schwarzenegger ultimately succeeded by appealing to independent voters and many labor and Latino Democrats; his campaign balanced the funds going to other candidates, especially from labor unions and tribal gaming interests, with nearly $9 million of his own money and massive free media.[15]

THE NEWS MEDIA AND CALIFORNIA POLITICS

From candidates and campaigns to public policy, almost everything Californians know about politics—which is not necessarily very much—comes from the news media. They have a profound impact on ideas, issues, and leaders. Until the 1950s, a few family-owned newspapers dominated the media. Then television gave the newspapers some competition while expanding the cumulative clout of the mass media. Today, new media like the Internet and a plethora of ethnic publications also play a role.

Paper Politics

California's great newspapers were founded in the nineteenth century by ambitious men such as Harrison Gray Otis of the *Los Angeles Times,* William Randolph Hearst of the *San Francisco Examiner,* and James McClatchy of the *Sacramento Bee*. These print-media moguls used their newspapers to boost their communities, their political candidates, and their favored causes. Most were like Otis, an ardent conservative who fought labor unions and pushed for growth while making a fortune in land investments. In the heyday of bosses and machines, his *Los Angeles Times* supported the Southern Pacific Railroad's political machine and condemned Progressive leader Hiram Johnson as a demagogue, as did many other newspapers in the state. Other journalists, however, helped found the Lincoln-Roosevelt League and led the campaign for reform.

After reform triumphed over the machine, newspapers continued to play a crucial role in California politics. In Los Angeles, San Francisco, Oakland, San Jose, and San Diego, Republican publishers used the power of the press—on editorial and news pages—to promote their favorite candidates and causes. They were instrumental in keeping Republicans in office long after the Democrats gained a majority of registered voters.

Change came in the 1970s, when most of California's family-owned newspapers became part of corporate chains. The new managers brought in more professional editors and reporters. News coverage became more objective, and opinion was more consistently confined to the editorial pages, which became distinctly less conservative.

Such editorials, expressing the opinion of the publisher or, more commonly, an editorial board made up of journalists, have been extremely influential in California politics. Voters often follow editorial recommendations on candidates and issues for lack of alternative sources of advice, especially on lower-profile races and ballot measures. For example, by winning newspaper editorials throughout the state, Larry Aceves, a little-known former school superintendent, beat two prominent legislators to come in first in the 2010 primary election for superintendent of public instruction. Despite these endorsements, however, he was defeated in the November election. Nevertheless, today's editorial pages are less influential than they once were as the number of newspapers and their circulation have declined.

At one time, there were hundreds of newspapers in California, with several competing with one another in most large cities. Today, less than a hundred survive, and most cities have just one. But that's not the only change. As a result of the loss of readers and advertisers to other media, the surviving newspapers have shrunk in both news coverage and staffing. The *Los Angeles Times,* for example, employed more than 1,300 journalists in 1998 but was down to 600 by 2009.[16] As a consequence of these changes, newspaper coverage of California politics is less extensive than it once was. Newspapers now share reporters or rely on the Associated Press or the *Los Angeles Times,* which still maintains the largest and most respected Sacramento bureau. Other media, including television and the Internet, have become more important to many people.

Television Politics

Public opinion surveys report that 37 percent of Californians say they get their news and information about state politics from television, with 15 percent citing newspapers, 10 percent radio, and 24 percent the Internet.[17] But television coverage of California politics leaves a lot to be desired.

Before Arnold Schwarzenegger was elected governor, not one of California's television stations, other than those based in Sacramento, operated a news bureau in the state capital. Television news editors avoided state political coverage because they believed that viewers wanted big national stories or local features. The minimal television coverage of state politics—a tiny percentage of newscast time, according to various studies—was mainly drawn from newspaper articles, wire service stories, or events staged by politicians, who struggled to gain any coverage at all. Even candidates for governor had a hard time making local news broadcasts, and most television stations declined to broadcast live candidate debates out of fear of low ratings. Cynics pointed out that if television doesn't provide news coverage, candidates are forced to buy advertising time—on television. As a consequence, candidate ads take up more time than news coverage of campaigns during the nightly news on California television stations—and provide a major source of revenue for the stations.

Nevertheless, television coverage of state politics has improved somewhat in the twenty-first century. A movie star governor and his carefully staged media events brought the cameras back to Sacramento. Coverage also increased with the advent of transmission by satellite vans, which made it easier for television stations to send reporters to cover breaking news and major events "live from the Capitol!" without the necessity of investing in permanent Sacramento bureaus. Ongoing conflict between the Republican governor and Democratic majorities in the legislature added drama, as did the state's persistent budget crisis.

Californians who prefer their politics raw—without reporters or commentary—can watch their government in action on the California Channel, now available on 114 cable systems.

New Media

The traditional print and broadcast media still dominate, but in recent years more alternative sources of news and information have become available to

Californians. Nearly seven hundred ethnic broadcasting outlets and publications now serve Californians in Spanish, Vietnamese, Mandarin, and many other languages.[18] Latino newspapers and television and radio stations reach major audiences, especially in Southern California. Many of these ethnic media are virtually obsessed with politics as their communities generate candidates or factional conflict.

Talk radio has also become a political fixture, especially in a state where people spend so much time in their cars. Fifty percent of Californians say they listen to opinion-filled radio shows "regularly" or "sometimes."[19] Politics is a hot topic on talk radio, which played a crucial role in stirring up the recall of Governor Gray Davis in 2003.

But the medium with the most spectacular recent impact on politics is the Internet. Access to news and information on the Internet has given audiences exponentially more information and sources and diverted audiences and advertisers from more traditional media, especially newspapers. Thousands of Web sites focus on state or local politics and give citizens direct access to their governments. Blogs by political junkies offer news and opinion and often break stories. Listservs and social networking keep members of traditional interest groups in touch with one another and create whole new communities. Seventy-five percent of Californians use a computer at home, work, or school, and 70 percent regularly use the Internet; 55 percent report that they get news on the Internet. Latinos, elders, and lower-income residents are less likely to have access to computers or use the Internet, however, so access is not equally distributed.[20]

ELECTIONS, CAMPAIGNS, AND THE MEDIA

The influence of money and the media is greater in California politics than in most other states. Politicians must organize their own campaigns, raise vast sums of money, and then take their cases to the people via direct mail and television. Such campaigns are inevitably personality oriented, with substantive issues taking a back seat to puff pieces or attacks on opponents. The media provide a check of sorts, but declining coverage limits its impact.

All of this takes us back to the issue of declining voter turnout. The recall election of 2003 and the presidential election of 2008 increased turnout, but only momentarily. Turnout in succeeding elections has been much lower. Could stronger parties, more news coverage, and public-financed, issue-oriented campaigns revive voter participation? Maybe, but campaign consultants and the media say they are already giving the public what it wants.

NOTES

1.   California Voter Foundation, "California Voter Participation Survey," March 2005, www.calvoter.org.

2.   "The Changing California Electorate," *California Opinion Index,* August 2009, www.fieldpoll.com (accessed June 27, 2010).

3. *Ibid.*

4. Ricardo Ramirez and Luis Fraga, "Continuity and Change: Latino Political Incorporation in California since 1990," in *Racial and Ethnic Politics in California,* ed. Sandra Bass and Bruce E. Cain (Berkeley: Berkeley Public Policy Press, Institute of Governmental Studies, University of California, 2008).

5. Public Policy Institute of California, "California's Likely Voters," *Just the Facts,* September 2009, www.ppic.org.

6. Public Policy Institute of California, "The Age Gap in California Politics," *Just the Facts,* August 2008, www.ppic.org.

7. National Association of Latino Elected Officials, "2010 Latino Electoral Profile: California State Primary Election," www.naleo.org (accessed June 28, 2010).

8. Gay and Lesbian Leadership Institute, www.glli.org/leadership (accessed June 27, 2010).

9. California Fair Political Practices Commission, "The Billion Dollar Money Train," April 2009, www.fppc.ca.gov (accessed June 29, 2010).

10. *Ibid.*

11. California Fair Political Practices Commission, "Independent Expenditures: The Giant Gorilla in Campaign Finance," June 2008, www.fppc.ca.gov (accessed June 29, 2010).

12. Dan Walters, "Proposition 34 Only Gave the Appearance of Reform," *San Jose Mercury News,* June 6, 2010. For more on how PACs shuffle funds and obscure sources, see "Campaign Spending Harder to Track," *San Jose Mercury News,* June 28, 2010.

13. "Capitol Weekly's Top 100 List, Parts I and II," *Capitol Weekly,* April 16 and 23, 2009, www.capitolweekly.net (accessed June 29, 2010).

14. "Whitman Digs Deep into Tech's Toolbox," *San Jose Mercury News,* July 2, 2010, p. 1A.

15. For a full discussion of the recall campaign, see Larry N. Gerston and Terry Christensen, *Recall! California's Political Earthquake* (Armonk, N.Y.: M. E. Sharpe, 2004).

16. "As Cities Downsize from Two Newspapers to Just One, Some Talk of Zero," *New York Times,* March 12, 2009.

17. Public Policy Institute of California, *Statewide Survey,* October 2010, www.ppic.org (accessed November 5, 2010).

18. Marcelo Ballve et al., *Profiles of Ethnic Media: California's New Civic Communicators* (San Francisco: New California Media, 2002).

19. Public Policy Institute of California, *Statewide Survey,* October 2004, www.ppic.org.

20. Public Policy Institute of California, *Statewide Survey,* June 2008, www.ppic.org.

LEARN MORE ON THE WEB

Public opinion polls:
    Public Policy Institute of California: www.ppic.org
    The Field Poll: www.fieldpoll.com

Elections, political reform, and campaign finance:
   California Secretary of State: www.sos.ca.gov
   California Fair Political Practices Commission: www.fppc.ca.gov
   California Voter Foundation: www.calvoter.org
   League of Women Voters: www.ca.lwv.org
   Smart Voter: www.smartvoter.org
   National Institute on Money in State Politics: www.followthemoney.org

News on state politics, campaigns, and elections:
   Capitol Weekly: www.capitolweekly.net
   California Report (radio): www.californiareport.org
   Rough & Tumble (links to news articles on California politics): www.
      rtumble.com

Listings of publications and broadcast media in California:
   ABYZ News Links: www.abyznewslinks.com/uniteca.htm
   California Voter Foundation: http://www.calvoter.org/issues/votereng/
      votpart/index.html

Blogs—for lively opinion and information on California politics:
   www.calbuzz.com
   www.calitics.com (progressive)
   www.californiarepublic.org (conservative)
   www.californiaprogressreport.com (progressive)
   www.flashreport.org (conservative)

LEARN MORE AT THE LIBRARY

Mark Baldassare. *A California State of Mind: The Conflicted Voter in a Changing World*. Berkeley: University of California Press, 2002. Developments in public opinion.

Greg Mitchell. *The Campaign of the Century*. New York: Random House, 1992. Upton Sinclair's 1934 campaign for governor.

Ethan Rarick, ed. *California Votes: The 2006 Governor's Race*. Berkeley: Berkeley Public Policy Press, Institute of Governmental Studies, University of California, 2007.

4

Interest Groups: The Power behind the Dome

CHAPTER CONTENTS

Many people belong to one or more **interest groups**—organizations formed to protect and promote the shared political objectives of their members. Existing in all shapes and sizes, interest groups range from labor unions, ethnic organizations, and business associations to student unions, environmental entities, and automobile clubs. Whatever their differences, interest groups share the same goal of seeing their visions and values incorporated into the actions of public policymakers.

In California, interest groups have prospered and proliferated, and in some ways cases become more important than political parties. That's because weak political parties and the state's election system provide a fertile political environment for organized groups to exercise influence. Weak political parties make candidates dependent on groups for financing, while direct democracy often enables groups to take their issues directly to the voters, circumventing the legislature and other elected policymakers in the process.

Interest groups come in all shapes and sizes. More people pay dues to the California Teachers Association (CTA) or the California Chamber of Commerce, for example, than contribute to the state Republican or Democratic parties. All groups are not equal, however; depending on resources and issues, some are far more successful than others. Just because groups are large does not automatically mean they are the most successful in having their way.

Besides exercising their influence through campaign contributions and use of direct democracy, interest groups also influence legislators in the lobbies beneath the capitol dome. Some observers view these efforts as assisting the legislative process; others see them as manipulating that process.

THE EVOLUTION OF GROUP POWER
IN CALIFORNIA

The astonishing length of California's constitution attests to the historical clout of the state's interest groups. In other states, groups gain advantages such as tax exemptions through acts of the legislature, which can be changed at any time. In California, such protections are often written into the constitution, making alteration difficult because constitutional amendments require the approval of the electorate. Among California's constitutionally favored interests are dozens of crops (protecting organized agriculture), trees less than forty years old (protecting the timber industry), and ships for passengers or freight (protecting the shipping industry). These "safeguards" were not responses to public demands. Instead, interest groups pushed them through for their own benefit either at the time the California Constitution was written or in subsequent elections.

Different interests have benefited throughout California's colorful history. In the early days, the mining industry and ranchers dominated the state's public policy environment. From about 1870 to 1910, the Southern Pacific Railroad monopolized California's economy and politics, with incredible control over both of California's major political parties.[1] Land development, shipping, and horse racing interests next dominated the political landscape through the mid-twentieth century, followed by the automobile and defense industries. Agricultural interests have remained strong through all these periods.

These days, banking and service businesses tower over manufacturing, while high-tech industries have surpassed defense and aerospace. Insurance companies, teachers' associations, physicians' and attorneys' groups, and other vocation-related associations also routinely lobby state government. Agribusiness also remains influential, particularly with respect to water policy and land use. Organized labor and business interests—almost always at odds—continue to battle for preeminence with the legislature and voters. They have been joined by the California Nations Indian Gaming Association, the largest contributor to the 2003 recall campaign and the largest contributor to a series of ballot propositions in 2008 that ratified gaming agreements between the tribes and the state. Single-issue groups, such as Gun Owners of California and Mothers Against Drunk Driving (MADD), have entered the fray, along with evangelical, pro-choice, right-to-life, minority, feminist, and gay and lesbian groups. Public interest groups, such as the League of Women Voters, Common Cause, and The Utility Reform Network (TURN), are also part of the ever-growing interest group mix. Pressured by these many groups and their financial contributions, California politicians often find themselves responding to the demands of interest groups rather than governing them.

THE GROUPS

Interest groups vary in size, resources, and goals. At one extreme, groups that pursue narrow and targeted economic benefits tend to have relatively small memberships but a great deal of financial resources. At the other end of the spectrum public interest groups often have large memberships but little money. A few, such as the Consumer Attorneys of California (CAC), whose membership consists of 3,000 trial lawyers, have the dual advantage of being both large and well funded. Others, such as the Consumers for Auto Reliability and Safety (CARS), operate on a shoestring.

Economic Groups

Economic groups that seek various financial gains or hope to prevent losses dominate the state's interest group environment. Every major corporation in the state, from Southern California Edison to the California Northern Railroad, is represented in Sacramento either by its own lobbyists or by lobbying firms hired to present the corporation's cases to policymakers. Often, individual corporations or businesses with similar goals form broad-based associations to further their general objectives. These umbrella organizations include the California Manufacturers and Technology Association, the California Business Alliance (for small enterprises), the California Bankers Association, and the California Council for Environmental and Economic Balance (for utilities and oil companies). The California Chamber of Commerce alone boasts 16,000 member companies that employ one-fourth of the private sector workforce in California.

Agribusiness is particularly active, because farming depends on the government on issues such as water availability and the regulation of pesticides. The giant farming operations maintain their own lobbyists, but various producer groups also form associations. Most of the state's winemakers, for example, are represented by the 850-member Wine Institute. The California Cotton Ginners Association has only 87 members, yet produces 750 million bales of cotton annually. Broader organizations, such as the California Farm Bureau Federation, one of the state's most powerful lobby groups, speak for agribusiness in general by representing 85,000 members with crops in excess of $36 billion in value.

Recently, high-tech industries have asserted their interests on issues ranging from Internet taxation and H–1B visas for foreign workers to transportation and public education. Organizations such as TechNet, the Silicon Valley Leadership Group, and the American Electronics Association have lobbied for regulatory changes, tax relief, research and development tax credits, "green" incentives in new areas such as solar energy, and other changes. The tech-heavy Silicon Valley Leadership Group alone represents 305 companies that provide $1.1 trillion worth of services and products in the global economy, exceeding the entire gross domestic product of India.[2]

Professional Associations and Unions

Professional associations such as the California Medical Association (CMA), the California Association of Realtors (CAR), and the Consumer Attorneys of California (CAOC) are among the state's most active groups, and they are regularly among the largest campaign contributors. Other professionals, such as chiropractors, dentists, and general contractors, also maintain active associations. Because all these professionals serve the public, many promote their concerns as broader than self-interest. Their credibility is further enhanced by expertise in their respective fields and by memberships consisting of affluent, respected individuals.

Teachers' associations and other public employee organizations fall somewhere between business associations and labor unions. Their members view themselves as professionals but in recent years have increasingly resorted to traditional labor union tactics, among them collective bargaining, strikes, and political campaign donations. Other public workers, including the highway patrol and state university professors, have their own organizations. The California State Employees Association (CSEA) is the giant among these groups, with more than 141,000 members and the ability to raise large campaign war chests for candidates and election issues.

Unions have done reasonably well in California, which ranks sixth among the fifty states in per capita union membership. Unions here represent 18 percent of the workforce, compared with 12 percent nationwide. Traditional labor unions represent nurses, machinists, carpenters, public utility employees, and dozens of other occupations. In 2002 unions worked to persuade the legislature to enact the nation's first paid family leave program, allowing workers to take leave from their jobs for up to six weeks at 55 percent of their salary or a maximum of $728 per week. In 2004 California became the first state in the nation to provide paid paternity leave. The new laws drew the wrath of the California Chamber of Commerce, which predicted that they would create hardship for businesses. Yet, only a fraction of those eligible to participate actually do so.[3]

Perhaps the most controversial union in state politics is the California Correctional Peace Officers Association (CCPOA), which contributed more than $600,000 to the reelection campaign of Governor Gray Davis in 2002, just before the governor signed a three-year pay increase of 35 percent in the midst of a huge state budget deficit. The agreement drew heated criticism of the union and

Davis, adding fuel to the recall accusation that Davis was little more than a tool of major contributors.[4] In 2004 Governor Arnold Schwarzenegger renegotiated the contract and won a slight modification in the pay raises, achieving only about one-third of the targeted savings. Still, the CCPOA is adept at looking out for its own interests. In 2008 the union funneled $1.8 million into a campaign to derail Proposition 5, which would have provided drug treatment and rehabilitation programs for many nonviolent drug offenders who otherwise would be sent to prison. The proposition failed, with 60 percent of the electorate voting against the measure.

Demographic Groups

Groups that depend more on membership numbers than on money can be described as **demographic groups**. Based on characteristics that distinguish their members from other segments of the population, such as their ethnicity, gender, or age, such groups usually have an interest in overcoming discrimination. Most racial and ethnic organizations fall into this category.

Virtually all of California's minorities have organizations that seek to be their voice. One of the earliest of these was the Colored Convention, which fought for the rights of African Americans in California in the nineteenth century. Today, several such groups advocate for African Americans, Asian Americans, and Native Americans. The United Farm Workers (UFW), GI Forum, Mexican American Legal Defense Fund (MALDEF), and Mexican American Political Association (MAPA) represent Latinos.

The National Organization for Women (NOW), EMILY's List (Early Money Is Like Yeast), and National Women's Political Caucus (NWPC) actively support women candidates and feminist causes. Unlike some of the other statewide organizations, these groups are better organized at the local level than at the state level, however.

Several organizations have become prominent over the definition of sexual equality. Gay rights groups have increased in numbers and voice in recent years, particularly over the issue of gay marriage. Equality California, the largest, has worked to elect gay legislators, obtain passage of equal rights legislation, and pursue gay marriage through both the courts and the legislative process. They have been opposed by groups like Campaign for California Families, which led the way to declare marriage as an act between a man and a woman in 2000 through **Proposition 22, the California in Defense of Marriage Act**. Californians have been battling over the issue ever since.

Age groups play a smaller part in state politics. California has an aging population heavily dependent on public services, however. Organizations such as AARP (formerly the American Association of Retired Persons), with no fewer than 3.3 million members in California, have achieved a higher profile in state politics, particularly on health-care issues.

Single-Issue Groups

The groups discussed so far tend to have broad bases and deal with a wide range of issues. Another type of interest group operates with a broad base of support for the resolution of narrow issues. **Single-issue groups** push for a specific question to be decided on specific terms. They support only candidates who agree with their particular position on an issue. The California Abortion Rights Action League (CARAL), for example, endorses only candidates who support a woman's right to choose (pro-choice), whereas antiabortion (or pro-life) groups such as the ProLife Council work only for candidates on the opposite side. Likewise, the Howard Jarvis Taxpayers Association evaluates candidates and ballot propositions solely in terms of whether they meet the association's objective of no unnecessary taxes and no wasteful government spending. Each of these groups exercises power on occasion, but their reluctance to compromise limits their effectiveness in the give-and-take of state politics.

A single-interest group's potential ability to deliver a solid bloc of voters on a controversial issue can affect the outcome of a close election and thus enhance its clout, at least on a temporary basis. That's what happened in 1982, when National Rifle Association (NRA) opposition to a proposed gun control initiative brought out sympathizers in droves and led to the defeat of antigun Democratic gubernatorial candidate Tom Bradley, who had been expected to win. An exception occurred in 2008, when antigay groups qualified and campaigned heavily for Proposition 8, a proposed constitutional amendment designed to overturn a state supreme court decision that had legalized same-sex marriage.[5] Advocates urged voters to use presidential candidate positions on the proposition as a guide to their votes. Barack Obama opposed the measure, yet he won California handily as the initiative squeaked by.

Public Interest Groups

Although virtually all organized interest groups claim to speak for the broader public interest, some groups clearly seek no private gain and thus more correctly can claim to be **public interest groups**. These groups are distinguished from other organizations by the fact that they pursue goals to benefit society, not just their members.

Some public interest groups, such as California OneCare, have been instrumental in the fight for health-care reform. Part of that organization's decade-long struggle was realized when Congress passed the Patient Protection and Affordable Care Act in 2010. Others, such as The Utility Reform Network (TURN), monitor rate requests by the utilities before the state Public Utilities Commission. In 2010 TURN led a coalition of consumer groups against PG&E–sponsored Proposition 16—a proposal that would have made it very difficult for municipalities to purchase renewable power.

Environmental organizations such as the Sierra Club and Friends of the Earth have been very active in California on issues such as water management, offshore oil drilling, air pollution, transportation, and pesticide use. Another important concern of these groups is land use, both for private development in sensitive areas and for public lands, which make up half the state. Surveys have reported that one in nine Californians claims membership in an environmental group.[6] The Sierra Club alone has more than 1.3 million members.

Other public interest groups, such as California Public Interest Research Group (CALPIRG), Common Cause, and the League of Women Voters, focus on governmental reform and voter participation. These groups have been involved in several efforts to reform campaign finance in California.

A final type of public interest group isn't really a group at all: local governments. Cities, school districts, special districts, and counties all lobby the state government—on whose funds they depend heavily—through the League of California Cities, the California School Boards Association (CSBA), and the California State Association of Counties (CSAC). Dozens of cities and counties employ their own lobbyists in Sacramento, as do other governmental agencies. One study found that local governments collectively spend more on lobbying than organized labor, oil companies, or businesses.[7] They also endorse ballot measures that affect their interests and, on rare occasions, even sponsor initiatives. Unlike other groups, cities and counties cannot make campaign contributions or organize their constituents, but they can make themselves heard. In 2010, local governments banded together to promote **Proposition 22, the Local Taxpayers, Public Safety and Transportation Act**, an initiative to keep the state government from borrowing or raiding funds that voters have dedicated to public safety.

TECHNIQUES AND TARGETS: INTEREST GROUPS AT WORK

Interest groups seek to influence public policy. To do this, they must persuade policymakers. The legislature, the executive branch, the courts, the bureaucracy, and sometimes the people are thus the targets of the various techniques these groups may use. Their primary weapons include lobbying, campaign support, litigation, and direct democracy.

Lobbying

The term **lobbying** refers to the activity that once went on in the lobbies adjacent to the legislative chambers. Advocates for various causes or issues would buttonhole legislators on their way in or out of the legislature and make their cases. This still goes on in the lobbies and hallways of the capitol, as well as in nearby bars and restaurants and wherever else policymakers congregate. Lobbyists are so integral to the legislative process that they are commonly referred to as members of the "third house," alongside the assembly and senate.

Until the 1950s, lobbying was a crude and completely unregulated activity. Lobbyists lavished food, drink, gifts, and money on legislators in exchange for favorable votes. Today's lobbyists, however, are experts on the legislative process. Many have served as legislators or staff for legislators. Often, they focus on legislative committees and leaders, lobbying the full legislature only as a last resort.

Unlike old-time lobbyists, today's advocates must be well informed to be persuasive. When inexperienced legislators are unable to grasp major issues, lobbyists fill the void, often by actually writing proposed legislation and assembling the coalitions of legislators necessary to pass it.[8] One study during the 2007–2008 legislative session found that 60 percent of the bills that became laws had been introduced by legislators on behalf of lobbyists.[9] Today's lobbyists still use money, but less cavalierly than in the past, instead strategically contributing to campaigns. Legislators and lobbyists alike assert that contributions buy access, not votes, but the tie between money and access can be powerful in its own right. "The bottom line," one strategist states, is that "the system favors the moneyed—and there's been no sign of political reform."[10] All of this makes lobbying not only a highly specialized profession but also an expensive activity. In fact, during 2009 lobby firms spent about $151 million just to influence the legislature alone—that averages out to $1.26 million per legislator.[11]

Although most lobbying activity is focused on the legislature, knowledgeable professionals also target the executive branch, from the governor down to the bureaucracy. The governor not only proposes the budget but also must respond to thousands of bills that await his or her approval or rejection. In the process, the governor frequently meets with lobbyists in an effort to come to terms on proposed legislation before it goes to the legislature.[12]

The roles and responsibilities of bureaucrats do not escape the attention of astute interest groups. The bureaucracy must interpret new laws and make future recommendations to the governor and legislature. Moreover, on questions ranging from tax exemptions to coastal access to energy regulations, bureaucrats often have the final say on how laws will work. One study on the implementation of AB 32, the Global Warming Solutions Act of 2006, found energy interests lobbying the California Air Resources Board more than the governor or legislature to gain favorable regulations. In the words of one energy lobbyist, "I'm not going to say we love the thing (AB 32), but if that's the way the state wants to go ... we want to make sure that we write regulations that we can comply with and are feasible to do."[13] Sometimes lobbyists will go so far as to offer "talking points" to help bureaucrats justify their decisions on public matters. "It's called 'spoon feeding,'" a lobbyist recently explained to a California coastal commissioner regarding a matter before the commission, "but we're happy to do it."[14]

Lately, the public has become a target of lobbying, too. In media-addicted California, groups have begun making their cases through newspaper and television advertising between elections. Health care, education, Indian gaming, and other issues have been subjects of costly media campaigns with the intent to motivate voters to communicate with state leaders.

Professional Lobbyists.   Between 1977 and 2007, the number of registered lobbyists in Sacramento nearly doubled, from 582 to 1,074, including about three dozen former legislators. That's about nine lobbyists per legislator. State law prevents former legislators from lobbying for one year after they leave office, but as one legislator has noted, "I would certainly be available to give people political advice."[15]

Most lobbyists represent a particular business, union, organization, or group. Others are **contract lobbyists**, advocates who work for several clients simultaneously. Whether contract or specialized, more and more lobbyists make a career of their professions, accruing vast knowledge and experience. These long-term professionals became even more powerful when term limits eliminated senior legislators with countervailing knowledge, although some lobbyists complain that term limits mean they must constantly reestablish their credibility with new decision makers. One prominent lobbyist, however, explains his lack of concern about term limits or other reforms: "Whatever your rules are, I'm going to win."[16]

Nonprofessional Lobbyists.   Some groups can't afford to hire a lobbyist, so they rely on their members instead. Even groups with professional help use their members on occasion to show elected officials the breadth of their support. Typically, this sort of lobbying is conducted by individuals who live in the districts of targeted legislators, although groups sometimes lobby en masse, busing members to the capitol for demonstrations or concurrent lobbying of many elected officials.

Such grassroots efforts by nonprofessionals have special credibility with legislators, but well-financed groups have learned to mimic grassroots efforts by forming front groups or "Astroturf" organizations that conceal their real interests. In 2008, for example, representatives of pornography filmmakers flooded the capitol for hearings on AB 2914, a bill that would have hiked taxes on the industry from 8 percent to 25 percent, adding $665 million to the beleaguered state coffers. Bill opponents included spokespersons from the Free Speech Coalition (FSC), an adult industry–funded group purportedly concerned with government efforts to limit free speech, regardless of the topic or issue. In this case, the FSC representatives argued that the tax would discriminate against those with different opinions. Through this vehicle, the porn industry appeared less self-serving and provided the logic for legislators to defeat the bill.

Campaign Support

Most groups also try to further their cause by helping sympathetic candidates win election and reelection, commonly through financial contributions to their campaigns. Groups with limited financial resources do so by providing volunteers to go door-to-door or to serve as phone-bank callers for candidates. Labor unions typically fall into this category, along with public education interests.

Groups with greater resources make generous campaign contributions. Sometimes such contributions appear to get the groups what they want. Take

TABLE 4.1 Top Ten Campaign Contributor Groups, 2008

Category	Money
Tribal governments	$163,223,555
Public-sector unions	37,926,398
Electric utilities	33,932,562
Oil and gas	25,491,497
Party committees	24,075,526
Gay/lesbian rights and issues	21,747,420
Candidate committees	18,115,167
General trade unions	17,075,442
Gambling and casinos	16,616,687
Real estate	15,408,393

SOURCE: Institute on Money in State Politics, www.followthemoney.org.

the issue of consumer protection from cell phone companies. Between 2006 and 2007, the legislature considered nine bills concerning billing transparency, contract grace periods, termination fees, and contract dispute rules. The industry opposed the bills as intrusive and unnecessary. Only one bill was signed to the law by the governor, while the rest never emerged from the legislature or were vetoed. Meanwhile, during the same period, the telecommunications industry pumped more than $7.2 million into political campaigns.[17] Table 4.1 illustrates the top ten interest group contributors in 2008.

Sometimes groups fail, no matter how much they contribute. In 2002 banks, insurance companies, and similar interests contributed more than $20 million in campaign contributions to defeat a bill by state senator Jackie Speier aimed at protecting the financial privacy of consumers.[18] Facing a similar outcome in 2003, Speier organized an initiative campaign and quickly collected 600,000 signatures; the moneyed interests retreated, and Speier's bill (SB1) was signed into law by Governor Davis. While they may not always succeed, powerful groups rarely hesitate to use their resources to tilt the outcomes in their favor.

Campaign contributors claim that their money merely buys them access to decision makers. The press and the public often suspect a more conspiratorial process, however, and evidence of money-for-vote trades has emerged in recent years. Federal Bureau of Investigation (FBI) agents posing as businesspeople asked legislators for favors in exchange for campaign contributions, resulting in the 1994 convictions of fourteen people, including five legislators. Their trials revealed the extent to which legislators hustle lobbyists for contributions. In another instance Chuck Quackenbush, California's elected insurance commissioner, was forced to resign in 2000 when it was discovered that he let insurance companies accused of wrongdoing avoid big fines by giving smaller amounts to foundations that subsequently spent the money on polls, ads featuring the commissioner, and other activities. And in 2005 Secretary of State Kevin Shelley resigned from his office after several allegations of illegal activities, including campaign contributions from a company that was awarded a major grant from his office.

As a result of these scandals, politicians and contributors probably exercise greater caution. The high cost of campaigning in California, though, means that candidates continue to ask and lobbyists and interest groups continue to give. Of significance, however, is that the campaign funds come from a variety of interest groups, as well as other sources.

Litigation

Litigation is an option when a group questions the legality of legislation, and in recent years many groups have turned to the courts for a final interpretation of the law. Groups have challenged state laws, regulations, and actions by the executive branch in court. In 2005, for example, the California Nurses Association successfully sued to force Governor Arnold Schwarzenegger to comply with a new state law that reduced the nurse-to-patient ratio. Although the governor lost that battle, he won another when he fended off a court challenge by the powerful California Teachers Association because he rescinded an earlier promise to return $2 billion he had denied the schools the previous year.

Over the years, interest groups have also raised legal challenges to several successful ballot measures—including measures on immigration, affirmative action, campaign finance, bilingual education, and same-sex marriage—hoping that the initiatives would be declared unconstitutional. Even if a group loses its case, it may be able to delay the implementation of a new law or at least establish a principle for debate in the future. In 2001 MALDEF challenged the legislature's redistricting plan, claiming underrepresentation of Latinos. Although the legislature's plan prevailed, MALDEF's tactic kept the issue on the public agenda throughout the decade.

Direct Democracy

In his 1911 inaugural address, Governor Hiram Johnson championed direct democracy to "place in the hands of the people the means by which they may protect themselves." He and his fellow Progressives envisioned the public as the ultimate custodian of the legislative process. A century later, however, only broad-based or well-financed groups have the resources to collect the necessary signatures or to pay for expensive campaigns. **Direct democracy** gives interest groups the opportunity to make policy themselves by promoting their proposals through initiatives and referenda.

Sometimes interest groups mobilize to gain passage of a ballot proposition; other times they work to defeat one. In 1998, for example, tribal supporters of gambling on Indian lands spent $10 million qualifying an initiative for the ballot in just thirty days—the most expensive petition campaign in history. The subsequent campaign on the proposition itself also broke records, with the two sides spending a total of $96 million. The voters ultimately approved the initiative. Since then, the costs have gone up. In 2008 the voters were asked to ratify four agreements allowing for 17,000 more slot machines in Indian casinos in addition to the 62,000 already in place, with projected annual taxes for the state at about $450 million. The pro-gaming interests spent more than $150 million on campaign activities—far exceeding the "no" side, which spent less than $40 million. The ballot propositions sailed through.

Big money was spent against two other initiatives in 2006. In one case the tobacco industry marshaled more than $65 million against Proposition 86, which sought to increase tobacco taxes by $2.60 per cigarette package (which would make California the highest tobacco-taxed state in the nation). Similarly, major oil companies spent more than $100 million in opposition to Proposition 87, an effort to tax oil profits with the proceeds used to pursue alternative-energy programs. The campaigns were successful, and the voters rejected both propositions.

But big money doesn't always win. For example, utility giant PG&E spent more than $3 million in 2010 gathering signatures for Proposition 16, the so-called Taxpayers Right to Vote Act. The proposal was actually a thinly veiled effort to change the state constitution to require any municipal power company to get a two-thirds vote of the people before buying renewable energy. PG&E poured more than $46 million into the effort against about $90,000 spent by the "no" side. The proposal was defeated, even though the opponents were outspent by a margin of 19,565 to 1.

The recall is also sometimes used by interest groups, usually to remove local elected officials. Teachers' unions, conservative Christians, and minority groups have conducted recall campaigns against school trustees, for example. These efforts, however, pale in comparison with the recall effort against Governor Gray Davis. The People's Advocate, a conservative antitax group, was among the leading forces early in that recall effort. During the campaign, groups ranging from the Howard Jarvis Taxpayers Association to the League of Conservation Voters weighed in on the issue.

REGULATING GROUPS

Free spending by interest groups and allegations of corruption led to the Political Reform Act of 1974 (introduced in Chapter 3), an initiative sponsored by Common Cause. Overwhelmingly approved by the voters, the law requires politicians to report their assets, disclose contributions, and declare how they spend campaign funds. Other provisions compel lobbyists to register with the secretary of state, file quarterly reports on their campaign-related activities, and reveal the beneficiaries of their donations. The measure also established the **Fair Political Practices Commission (FPPC)**, an independent regulatory body, to monitor these activities. When the commission finds incomplete or inaccurate reporting, it may fine the violator. Of greater concern than the financial penalty, however, is the bad press for those who incur the commission's reprimand.

The voters approved new constraints in 1996, when they enacted strict limits on interest groups' practice of rewarding supportive legislators with travel and generous fees for speeches. However, this legislation was soon challenged, creating an atmosphere of uncertainty. In 2000 voters approved yet another initiative, **Proposition 34**, which placed new constraints on political action committees and attempted to limit contributions to political campaigns. Yet between self-financed campaigns and the vigorous activities of groups engaged in independent expenditures, any thoughts of reduced spending quickly vanished.

MEASURING GROUP CLOUT: MONEY, NUMBERS, AND CREDIBILITY

Campaign regulations are generally intended to reduce the disproportionate influence of moneyed interests in state politics, but economic groups still have the advantage. Their money makes the full panoply of group tactics available to them and gives them the staying power to outlast the enthusiasm and energy of grassroots groups. The California Chamber of Commerce, for example, contributes lavishly to legislative campaigns and has been a major source of funds for Arnold Schwarzenegger, the first gubernatorial candidate endorsed by the Chamber in its 115-year history. Between 2004 and 2008 the Chamber listed fifty-one "job killer" bills that would be harmful to California business that reached the governor's desk; forty-seven were vetoed by Governor Schwarzenegger. Allan Zaremberg, president of the Chamber, attributes this to the "parallel agendas" of the governor and his organization, but campaign contributions and effective lobbying surely helped.[19] Of course, when Gray Davis was governor, labor unions enjoyed much the same kind of special relationship. Some interest groups are always likely to be more successful than others.

Public interest groups and demographic groups, however, gain strength from numbers, credibility, and motives other than self-interest. Occasionally they prevail, such as in 1998, when children's groups and health groups overcame a financial disadvantage to pass Proposition 10, a cigarette tax dedicated to children's health programs, and in 2010, when financially impotent public interest groups won the Proposition 16 battle against PG&E. More commonly, interest groups affected by potentially harmful new costs rise to the occasion, as was the case in 2006, when the oil and tobacco industries spent nearly $200 million and reversed public opinion—and the votes—on measures to tax oil and increase tobacco taxes.

How powerful are interest groups and their lobbyists? It's hard to tell, but one informal survey of twelve first-time legislators reported that lobbyists wrote 70 percent of the bills they proposed.[20] Whatever the balance among groups, they are central to California politics. In a political environment characterized by weak political parties and direct democracy, California's myriad interests have plenty of opportunity to thrive.

NOTES

1. See Stephanie S. Pincetl, *Transforming California: A Political History of Land Use and Development* (Baltimore, MD: The Johns Hopkins University Press, 1999), pp. 20-22.

2. *CEO Business Climate Survey, 2008* (San Jose, Calif.: Silicon Valley Leadership Group, 2009), p. 2.

3. *California Business Issues, 2004* (Sacramento: California Chamber of Commerce, 2004), p. 77; also see "Few Take State's Family Leave," *San Jose Mercury News*, July 4, 2006, pp. 1C, 9C.

4. See Larry N. Gerston and Terry Christensen, *Recall! California's Political Earthquake* (Armonk, NY: M. E. Sharpe), 2004, p. 22.

5. The ruling was *In re Marriage Cases*, S147999.

6. Public Policy Institute of California, *Statewide Survey*, June 2000, www.ppic.org.

7. "Cities, Counties, Pay Price for Capitol Clout," *Los Angeles Times*, September 10, 2007, pp. B1, B4.

8. See "Bumper Crop of Clout*," Los Angeles Times*, September 22, 2004, pp. A1, A22, A23.

9. "How Our Laws Are Really Made," *San Jose Mercury News*, July 11, 2010, pp. A1, A6, A7.

10. "Special Interests: How They Get around Voter-Approved Limits on Campaign Contributions," *San Francisco Chronicle*, February 11, 2008, pp. A1, A6.

11. "End of Session Money Rains Down on Candidates," press release, California Fair Political Practices Commission, September 16, 2009.

12. See "A Lobbyist by Any Other Name?" *San Jose Mercury News*, May 20, 2005, pp, 1A, 17A.

13. "Lobbyists Heat up over Climate Law," *Sacramento Bee*, July 12, 2010, pp. A1, A10.

14. "E-mails Put California Coastal Commissioner in an Awkward Spot," *Los Angeles Times*, July 10, 2010, p. AA3.

15. "Elective Office Improves a Resume," *Los Angeles Times*, November 24, 2006, pp. B1, B11.

16. Douglas Foster, "The Lame Duck State," *Harper's*, February 1994.

17. See "Cell Phone Lobby Thwarts Reform Efforts," *San Jose Mercury News*, September 18, 2007, pp. 1A, 15A.

18. "$20 Million Tab to Defeat a Privacy Bill," *San Francisco Chronicle*, September 7, 2002, pp. A1, A11.

19. "Business Czar Delivers Major Cash to Governor," *San Jose Mercury News*, February 22, 2005, pp. 1A, 12A; also see "Business Sees an Ally in Governor," *Los Angeles Times*, October 18, 2004, pp. B1, B7.

20. Foster, *op. cit.*

LEARN MORE ON THE WEB

California Association of Realtors (CAR):
www.car.org

California Chamber of Commerce:
www.calchamber.com

California Labor Federation:
www.calaborfed.org

Common Cause:
www.commoncause.org

Howard Jarvis Taxpayers Association:
www.hjta.org

Latino Issues Forum:
www.lif.org

League of Women Voters of California:
www.ca.lwv.org

Sierra Club:
www.sierraclub.org/ca

LEARN MORE AT THE LIBRARY

Mark Arax and Rick Wartzman. *The King of California*. New York: Public Affairs Press, 2003.

Derek Cressman. *The Recall's Broken Promise: How Big Money Still Runs California Politics*. Sacramento, CA: The Poplar Institute, 2007.

Frank Norris. *The Octopus*. New York: Doubleday and Company, 1901.

Stephanie S. Pincetl. *Transforming California: A Political History of Land Use and Development*. Baltimore, MD: The Johns Hopkins University Press, 1999.

Arthur H. Samish and Bob Thomas. *The Secret Boss of California*. New York: Crown Books, 1971.

Dan Walters and Jay Michael. *The Third House*. Berkeley: Berkeley Public Policy Press, Institute of Governmental Studies, University of California, 2002.

5

The Legislature: The Perils of Policymaking

CHAPTER CONTENTS

Thousands of bills are introduced in the California legislature every year. Some are narrow in focus, such as requiring egg-laying chickens to have enough room to walk in their cages (passed in 2010) or a truth-in-advertising law about pomegranate juice (passed in 2009). Others, such as sweeping telecommunications legislation (passed in 2010) or mortgage fraud legislation (passed in 2009) attempt to settle disputes between competing industries that have a great deal of resources at stake. Some of these laws may seem a waste of time to the casual observer, although they usually are critically important to the constituencies they affect.

But along with deciding relatively obscure matters removed from the public eye, the legislature is responsible for solving the state's thorniest problems, including underfunded public education, inadequate revenues, the need for environmental protection, a decaying infrastructure, and an ever-fraying social safety net. Each year the members write thousands of laws and, along with the governor, determine the budget and fund services and programs. As a focal point of power, the legislature is a natural target of public scrutiny, and criticism of it is understandable. Less understandable, however, is its inability to resolve big issues in a contentious political environment.

Of course, the legislature does not act in a policymaking vacuum; rather, it must share power with the other branches of government. Nowhere has there been more disdain for that requirement than in the relationship between the legislature and the governor. For the last twenty-five years, California governors and the legislature have tangled on a regular basis. During that period, the legislature has rarely enacted the state budget before the start of the fiscal year on July 1. In addition, the legislature has suffered internally due to political—and philosophical—battles not only between Democrats and Republicans, but also internally between assembly Democrats and senate Democrats and assembly Republicans and senate Republicans. As one beleaguered assembly member said during lengthy budget negotiations, "More times than not, it seems that we have four political parties in the legislature alone!" Partisanship and ideological schisms drape the legislative process in California in ways rarely observed elsewhere, and these stark divisions often leave the body tied in political knots.

Then there's the question of public policy priorities. Some observers have wondered in recent years how the legislature could immerse itself in issues such as tanning salon rules for teenagers and imported kangaroo leather regulations, yet seemingly avoid questions about tax reform, water policy, and universal health insurance. It's no wonder that a 2010 public opinion survey found a whopping 75 percent of likely voters critical of the state legislature—a disapproval rating even higher than that of Governor Arnold Schwarzenegger.[1] Still, the legislature was established as the state institution most directly linking the people with their government. The question is, Does it still do its job in the twenty-first century?

THE MAKING AND UNMAKING OF A MODEL LEGISLATURE

Structurally and numerically, much of today's state legislature parallels its original design and intent. But a series of circumstances in the state's political environment have left the legislative branch considerably different than its national counterpart.

A Little History

California's first constitution, in 1849, provided a **bicameral (two-house) legislature** similar to the U.S. Congress. When the constitution was revised thirty years later, the senate was fixed at forty members serving four-year terms (with half the body elected every two years), and the assembly was set at eighty members serving two-year terms. Those numbers and terms of office continue to this day. Throughout the first hundred years of governance, legislators met on a part-time basis, with budgets crafted in two-year increments—characteristics that would change over time.

Beginning in 1926, the organization of the legislature paralleled that of the U.S. Congress. Assembly members, like their counterparts in the U.S. House of Representatives, were elected on the basis of population, and senators were elected by county in the same way that each state has two U.S. senators.[2] The large number of lightly populated counties north of the Tehachapi Mountains enabled the rural north to dominate the state senate despite Southern California's growth. By 1965, twenty-one of the forty state senators in California represented only 10 percent of the population; Los Angeles County, then home to 35 percent of the state's residents, had but a single state senator.

The Shift toward Professionalism

Then came change. The United States Supreme Court's **Reynolds v. Sims** decision in 1964 ordered all states to organize their upper houses by population rather than by county or territory. In California, the shift increased urban and southern representation dramatically, with rural and northern representation experiencing a corresponding decline. The revised method of organization produced numerous consequences—some intended, some not. The new legislators were younger, better educated, and more ideological, and more of them were members of racial minorities. More women also were elected. The transition to modernity was completed in 1966, when the voters created a full-time legislature with full-time salaries.

These days, the legislature meets an average of more than two hundred days per year, with full-time salaries to match. As of 2011, their base salary is $95,291—down from the $116,208 that legislators collected until the most recent recession, but still the highest among the fifty states. Perks push annual incomes close to $140,000.[3] Only nine other states have full-time legislatures.[4]

Redistricting: Keeping and Losing Control

By law, every ten years after the national census, the state realigns congressional and state legislative districts so that all have the same population. This process is known as **redistricting**. As of January 1, 2010, the California State Demographics Unit (the state equivalent to the U.S. Census Bureau) estimated California's population at 38,600,000. The state's population grows unevenly. So, during 2011, the state's new fourteen-member **Citizens Redistricting Commission** must realign legislative districts to be equal in size once again—482,500 for each assembly district and 965,000 in each senate district. This task is a first of its kind in California.

FIGURE 5.1 Map of State Senate District 15

Until 2011, redistricting had been left to the legislature, as is the case in most states. But in recent years, critics charged the legislature with being more intent on self-preservation than on providing compact geographic boundaries. After completion of the 2001 redistricting process, one senate district was two hundred miles in length, while others appeared almost as a Rorschach inkblot personality test. Figures 5.1 and 5.2 show examples of the legislature's work. As a result, the partisan compositions of the legislature remained almost identical throughout the decade. Some observers attacked the 2001 redistricting plan as an "incumbency protection plan" that needlessly split cities and ignored natural communities.[5] They argued that packing districts with disproportionate numbers of Democrats

FIGURE 5.2 Map of State Assembly District 60

or Republicans reduced competition. As one legislator complained, "What happened to drawing lines for the people of the state rather than ourselves?"[6]

Governor Arnold Schwarzenegger campaigned to establish a redistricting commission of retired judges in a 2005 special election, but the voters soundly rejected his proposal after legislative leaders promised to come up with a better plan. They never did. In 2008, Schwarzenegger joined with Common Cause, the League of Women Voters, and other reform groups to craft **Proposition 11, the Voters FIRST Initiative**. The ballot proposal placed redistricting in the hands of a fourteen-member independent commission. This time, the voters approved the measure, which takes effect before the 2012 state elections. But the redistricting battle has not gone away. Legislative supporters placed the redistricting issue before the voters again in 2010 with Proposition 27, the Financial Accountability in Redistricting Act. However, the voters were content to try the independent commission concept and rejected the proposal. With a new redistricting system in place, it remains to be seen whether the legislature will

TABLE 5.1 Political Parties in the State Legislature, 1981–2011

Legislative Session	Senate			Assembly	
	Democrats	Republicans	Independents	Democrats	Republicans
1981–1982	23	17		48	32
1983–1984	25	14	1	48	32
1985–1986	25	15		47	33
1987–1988	24	15	1	44	36
1989–1990	24	15	1	47	33
1991–1992	27	12	2	47	33
1993–1994	23	15	2	49	31
1995–1996	21	17	2	39	41
1997–1998	22	17	1	42	38
1999–2000	25	15		48	32
2001–2002	26	14		50	30
2003–2004	25	15		48	32
2005–2006	25	15		48	32
2007–2008	25	15		48	32
2009–2010	25	15		50	30
2011–2012	25	13		52	28

SOURCE: California Secretary of State.

become less partisan and more effective. Table 5.1 displays the partisan break-down of the legislature since 1981.

Term Limits

Much of the legislature's recent look stems from rising voter antipathy toward incumbents and the near certainty of their perpetual reelection. In 1990 the voters passed **Proposition 140**, an initiative that limited elected executive branch officers and state senators to two 4-year terms and assembly members to three 2-year terms, while reducing the legislature's operating budget (and thus its staff) by 38 percent. Clearly, California voters thought their legislature had become too professional for its own good.

Term-limits advocates envisioned a "turnstile" type of legislature, with members in office for relatively short periods. The system was designed to guarantee new faces, reduce the influence of money, and prevent incumbents from becoming entrenched in excess. Of the fifteen states currently with term-limit legislation in place, California is tied with Arkansas and Michigan for the strictest conditions in the nation. Once legislators complete their terms of service, they may never run for election again.

Some objectives associated with **term limits** have been met, while others show no sign of coming to pass. New faces have certainly appeared—particularly women and minorities in much larger numbers than in the past—but in many cases legislators have simply jumped from one house to the other. And at least one study shows that the most common vocational backgrounds of legislators before term limits—law and business—remain the dominant career patterns in the term-limits era.[7] Those from relatively affluent backgrounds continue be disproportionately elected to the legislature. In this sense, little has changed.

There also have been increasing instances of political cannibalism. In some cases, **termed-out** assembly members have challenged senators from their own political party who are eligible to serve another term. In other cases, senators who have a term left in the assembly have attempted to return to that house. In other instances still, termed-out legislators have returned to their counties to run for county supervisor. The term-limits concept in California has spawned the state's version of "musical chairs."

Although the flow of money into campaign coffers has been slowed, the overall costs of campaigning continue to set new records. Research also reveals that another significant impact of term limits has been a considerable decline in the quality of legislation in the postlimits era.[8]

Another criticism of term limits centers on the loss of legislative knowledge because of the rapid turnover. Because legislators have little opportunity to gain expertise, they tend to rely more on the governor and lobbyists,[9] the former because of the governor's access to the bureaucrats who advise him or her and experts who work as aids in the governor's office, and the latter because of the permanence of the lobbyists in the state capital. Legislators may be termed out, but lobbyists are not.

Meanwhile, leadership positions in the legislature no longer carry the clout that once made that branch an effective counterweight to the executive branch. Karen Bass, for example, who was elected speaker of the assembly in 2008, was termed out of the assembly as of 2010. John Perez, her successor, was elected to the assembly's highest post with only a year of experience under his belt. Both approaches show the problems that can develop with erratic leadership changes.

Nationwide, the term limits movement seems to be abating. Mississippi voters rejected the concept in 1999. In 2002, the Idaho legislature removed term limits, and the Oregon Supreme Court found the state law on term limits unconstitutional. In 2003, the Utah state legislature repealed term limits in that state. But in California, the voters continue to favor term limits. A public opinion poll in 2009 found that a resounding 65 percent of Californians supported the concept.[10]

New Rules, New Players

Redistricting, the change from part-time to full-time legislators, higher salaries, and term limits transformed the legislature, albeit unevenly. To be sure, the new framework attracted better-educated and more professional individuals and also made election to office more feasible for women and minorities. Thus, in 2011,

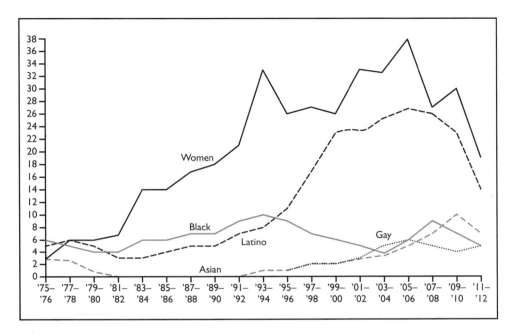

FIGURE 5.3   Women and Minorities in the California Legislature

the assembly included 19 women, 14 Latinos, 5 African Americans, 7 Asian Americans, and 5 openly gay members; the senate included 13 women, 10 Latinos, 2 African Americans, 2 Asian Americans, and 2 openly gay members. (see Figure 5.3).

Despite greater diversity, the legislature has narrowed in terms of vocational backgrounds. During the 1980s, legislative aspirants from the business world were flanked by large numbers of lawyers, local activists, educators, and former legislative aides. But increasingly, the "business candidate" has emerged as the dominant category of self-description. During the 1990s, about half of all legislative candidates on the ballot listed some form of business as their occupation. Beginning in the late 1990s, large numbers of people from city- and county-elected posts also took seats in the legislature.[11] These patterns continue today.[12]

LEADERS AND STAFF MEMBERS

Although the two houses share lawmaking responsibilities, they function differently. Because the assembly is larger, it is more hierarchical in organization. The **speaker of the assembly** is clearly in charge of that body and wields considerable power. The speaker controls the flow of legislation, designation of committee chairs and assignments, and distribution of vast campaign funds to the members of his or her political party. The number of standing, or topical, committees varies each term with the speaker's term in office. For example, there were thirty such committees in the assembly during 2009–2010, one more than in the previous session. Some committees are far more important than others, so the speaker's friendship is of great value to a legislator. The speaker also may carry favor with the governor, especially if the two work well together.

By tradition, the party with a majority in the assembly chooses the speaker in a closed meeting, or caucus. A vote is then taken by the full assembly, with the choice already known to all. The minority party selects its leader in a similar fashion. Majority and minority floor leaders, as well as their whips (assistants), provide further support for the legislative officers. With solid majorities for most of the past half-century, the Democrats have controlled the speakership for all but four years during the period.

Before the term-limits era, speakers often held their posts for ten years or more. However, since 1996—the year when term limits set in—the tenures of speakers have been limited to between one and three years. The current speaker, John Perez, may stretch that life span a bit. He was elected to his post in 2009 and may serve through 2014, assuming he is re-elected.

Prior to the court-ordered redistricting in 1966, the senate emphasized collegiality and cooperation over strong leadership, strict rules, and tight organization. Since the late 1960s, the senate has operated with a level of partisanship closer to that found in the assembly. The most powerful member is the **president pro tem**, who, like the speaker, is elected by the majority party after each general election. The minority party also elects its leader at that time. The key to senate power lies with the five-member **Rules Committee**, or **Senate Rules Committee**, which is chaired by the president pro tem and controls all other committee assignments and the flow of legislation. In 2009–2010 the senate had twenty-three standing committees, the same number as the previous session.

When Democrat John Burton presided as the pro tem, he used the office to raise and dispense large sums of money to grateful fellow Democrats. Burton was president pro tem for six years (1998–2004). More significantly, he had been an assembly member for nearly twenty years, mostly before the term-limits era. Because of his experience, Burton became the legislature's lightning rod against Governor Arnold Schwarzenegger. Many observers viewed him as the legislature's most formidable leader, despite the assembly speaker's traditionally dominant role.

The current president pro tem, Darrell Steinberg, was elected to the position in 2008. He will not be termed out until 2014. Like most others in leadership positions, Steinberg assumed his post with relatively little experience, although he did serve six years in the state assembly.

Although Democrats hold leadership positions in both houses, in recent years they have had as much trouble dealing with one another as they have had with Republican governor Schwarzenegger. Some of this trouble may be due to the differing leadership styles of Senate President Pro Tem Steinberg and Assembly Speaker Perez. Steinberg has a record of crossing party lines to forge necessary, if distasteful, compromises. Perez has a reputation for being unwilling to part with core values.[13] Their internal gridlock has taken considerable pressure off the minority Republicans, who have watched internal struggles within the majority party with some glee. Nowhere has this been more evident than in the struggle to balance annual state budgets facing huge deficits. As the legislature grappled with its responsibilities in 2010, interest groups loyal to both sides actually began letter-writing campaigns and purchased television ads—all of which points to the lack of cohesion within the political parties.[14]

STAFFING THE PROFESSIONAL LEGISLATURE

The evolution of the legislature into a full-time body was accompanied by a major expansion of its support staff. In 1990 the number of legislative assistants totaled 2,400—a far cry from the 485 employed by the last part-time legislature in 1966. Reductions from Proposition 140 pared the number of staffers to about 1,750, although increases in the state's population have led to a slow increase in the number of positions. As of 2010, about 2,500 staffers worked for the legislature. Those in the capital usually concentrate on pending legislation and research, whereas staffers in the legislators' home district offices spend much of their time responding to constituents' problems. The efforts of these staffers help each legislator to remain in good standing with his or her district.

Legislators spend much of their time in committees, the heart of the legislative process. Most committees cover specialized policy areas such as education or natural resources. A few, such as the senate and assembly rules committees, deal with procedures and internal organization. Each committee employs staff consultants who are experts on the committee's subject area and who are politically astute individuals in general—important attributes because they serve at the pleasure of the committee chair. Besides the traditional or standing committees, staffers assist more than sixty select committees that address narrow issues and nine joint committees that coordinate two-house policy efforts.

Another staff group is even more political. Employed by the Democratic and Republican caucuses and answering to the party leaders in the senate and assembly, these assistants are supposed to deal with possible legislation. However, their real activities usually center on advancing the interests of their party.

In addition to personal, committee, and leadership staffers, legislators have created neutral support agencies. With a staff of fifty-two, the **legislative analyst** (a position created in 1941) provides fiscal expertise, reviewing the annual budget and assessing programs that affect the state's coffers. The **legislative counsel** (created in 1913) employs about eighty attorneys to draft bills for legislators and determine their potential impact on existing legislation. The **state auditor** (created in 1955) assists the legislature by periodically reviewing ongoing programs.

Historically, staffing has enhanced the legislature's professionalism. Yet some staffers, especially those who work for the legislative leaders, clearly spend more time on partisan politics than on legislation. Many have used their positions as apprenticeships to gain knowledge, skills, and contacts for their own campaign efforts. All this, critics point out, is funded by the taxpayers. Defenders of the system counter that this staffing system helps compensate for weak party organizations and the information gaps associated with rapid legislative turnover.

HOW A BILL BECOMES A LAW

The legislature passes laws. It also proposes constitutional amendments, which may be submitted for voter approval after they receive absolute two-thirds majority votes in both houses (the votes of two-thirds of the full membership—that is, twenty-seven votes in the senate and fifty-four in the assembly). The same absolute two-thirds majority votes are required for the legislature to offer bond measures—money borrowed for long-term, expensive state projects. Proposed bond measures must then obtain majority votes at the next election before becoming law.

Most of the legislature's energy, however, is spent on lawmaking. Absolute majorities—twenty-one votes in the senate and forty-one votes in the assembly—are required to pass basic laws intended to take effect the following January, but absolute two-thirds votes in both houses are required for appropriations, urgency measures (those that become law immediately upon the governor's signature), and overrides of the governor's veto. The process, however, is far from simple.

The Formal Process

The legislative process begins when the assembly member or senator sponsoring a bill gives the clerk of the chamber a copy, which is recorded and numbered (see Figure 5.4). The process is known as moving the bill "across the desk" (of the receiving clerk), signifying that the proposed measure is now officially under consideration. The bill then undergoes three readings and several hearings before it is sent to the other house, where the process is repeated. The first reading simply acknowledges the bill's submission.

Depending upon the bill's origin, either the senate Rules Committee or the assembly Rules Committee decides on the route of the bill. The chairs of these important committees can affect a bill's fate by sending it to "friendly" or "hostile" committees and by assigning it a favorable or unfavorable route. Typically, a bill is assigned to two or three committees for careful scrutiny by members who are experts in that bill's subject area. More than half of all bills die in committee, either through a formal vote or because the chair decides not to call for a vote.

More than six thousand bills are introduced during each two-year session, with assembly members limited to fifty proposals and senators limited to sixty-five. With such volume, the **legislative committees** are essential to getting laws passed. They hold hearings, debate, and may eventually vote on each bill delegated to them. Most committees deal in narrow areas, but a few—such as the senate Budget and Fiscal Review Committee and the assembly Committee on

Appropriations—focus on the collection and distribution of funds and thus enjoy clout that goes beyond any one policy area.

At the conclusion of its hearings, a committee can kill a bill, release it without recommendation, or approve it with a "do pass" proposal. It may also recommend approval contingent on certain changes or amendments, which can be substantial or minor and technical. Only when a bill receives a positive recommendation from all of the committees to which it was assigned is it likely to get a second reading by the full legislative body. At this stage, the house considers additional amendments. After all proposed revisions have been discussed, the bill is printed in its final form and presented to the full house for a third reading. After further debate on the entire bill, a vote is taken.

Sometimes, the bill changes so dramatically that the original author abandons sponsorship in disgust; the bill then dies unless another legislator assumes sponsorship. On other occasions, a bill is introduced about a topic of little significance or with little more than a number. Then, later in the term, when the deadline for introductions has passed, the author may strip the bill of its original language and offer replacement language to deal with a pressing topic new to the legislative agenda. This strategy, known as **gut-and-amend**, isn't pretty, but gives a legislator flexibility he or she would not have otherwise. It also circumvents the normal legislative process of committee hearings and due deliberation, much to the chagrin of some lobbyists and interest groups.

If a bill is approved by the members of one house, it goes to the other house, where the process starts anew. Again, the bill may die anywhere along the perilous legislative path. If the two houses pass different versions of the same bill, the versions must be reconciled by a **conference committee**. Senate members are appointed by the Rules Committee; assembly members are chosen by the speaker, yet another sign of the power that comes with that position. If the conference committee agrees on a single version and if both houses approve it by the required margins, the bill goes to the governor for his or her approval. Otherwise, the proposed legislation is dead.

Usually, a bill becomes law if the governor signs it or takes no action within twelve days. However, if it is passed immediately before a session's end, the governor has thirty days to act. If the governor vetoes a bill, an absolute two-thirds majority must be attained in both houses for it to become law. Attaining such a lopsided vote is next to impossible, so vetoed bills generally fall by the wayside.

The Informal Process

Politics permeates the formal, "textbook" process by which a bill becomes law. This means that every piece of legislation is considered not only on its merits but also on the basis of a variety of factors, including political support, interest group pressure, public opinion, and personal power.

Members of the majority party chair most, if not all, of the committees in any given year. With Democrats in control for most of the last five decades, they have reaped the benefits of the committee chairs (extra staff, procedural advantages, and so forth), secured the best committee assignments, and been assigned

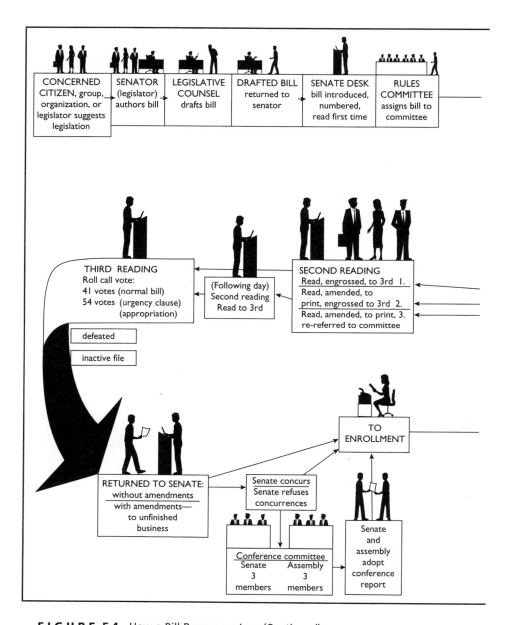

| CONCERNED CITIZEN, group, organization, or legislator suggests legislation | SENATOR (legislator) authors bill | LEGISLATIVE COUNSEL drafts bill | DRAFTED BILL returned to senator | SENATE DESK bill introduced, numbered, read first time | RULES COMMITTEE assigns bill to committee |

THIRD READING
Roll call vote:
41 votes (normal bill)
54 votes (urgency clause)
(appropriation)

defeated

inactive file

(Following day)
Second reading
Read to 3rd

SECOND READING
Read, engrossed, to 3rd 1.
Read, amended, to
print, engrossed to 3rd 2.
Read, amended, to print, 3.
re-referred to committee

RETURNED TO SENATE:
without amendments
with amendments—
to unfinished
business

Senate concurs
Senate refuses
concurrences

TO ENROLLMENT

Conference committee
Senate   Assembly
3   3
members   members

Senate
and
assembly
adopt
conference
report

FIGURE 5.4 How a Bill Becomes a Law (Continued)

the best offices. Likewise, when assembly Republicans briefly held a bare majority in 1996, they assumed control of twenty-five of the twenty-six committees,
and the benefits were reversed.

Political support within the legislature is essential to numerous decisions. So
many bills flow through the process that members often vote on measures they
haven't even read, relying on staff, committee, or leadership recommendations.
Sometimes, a bill's fate rests with key legislative leaders, who can use their

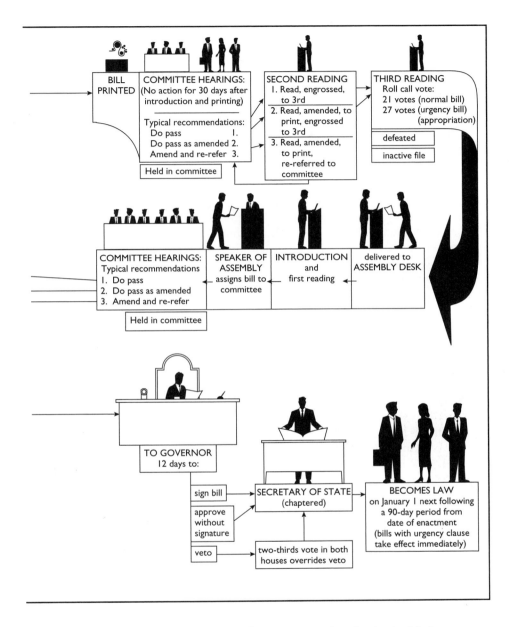

positions to stifle or speed up a proposal at various points in the legislative process. In the assembly, the speaker may actually appoint extra members to a committee temporarily to move a bill along. Outcomes are also affected by **logrolling**, a give-and-take bargaining process in which legislators agree to support each other's bills. More often than not, legislators give away their votes on matters of little concern to them in hopes of mollifying opponents or pleasing powerful leaders. And on occasion, some members of the assembly have been known to cast the votes of other members by clicking their electronic devices.

This illegal activity, called **ghost voting**,[15] can't take place in the senate, where members cast votes by a show of hands.

Public opinion also affects legislation, sometimes dramatically. Recent statutes on excessive drinking, smoke-free restaurants and bars, environmental quality, and longer sentences for repeat felons have been enacted in direct response to public concern.

As noted in Chapter 4, pressure from interest groups permeates the legislative process. With the combined cost of legislative campaigns leaping from $7 million in 1966 to $100 million in 1998, candidates welcomed the contributions of these interest groups. Proposition 34, enacted in 2002, attempted to impose some constraints on such fund-raising. Thus, in 2002 the cost of state legislative campaigns declined to $76.5 million.[16] Nevertheless, by 2008 the cost of state legislative campaigns had grown by more than 60 percent, to $129.75 million.[17] At just under $1.3 million per seat (eighty assembly, twenty state senate), California's legislative elections were the most expensive in the nation. And given the millions of dollars spent by independent expenditure committees that were not tied officially to any candidate, the total spent on legislative campaigns in the state in all likelihood exceeded $150 million.

OTHER FACTORS

Finally, personal power within the legislature remains a component of the political process, especially in cases of conflict. One such example occurred in 2008, when then senate president pro tem Don Perata and the Democratic majority of the senate Rules Committee blocked four Schwarzenegger nominees to the twelve-member California Parole Board. For months, Perata had complained about California's low parole rate, implying that the problem rested with the parole board. This action sent a clear message to both the board and the governor.[18]

Sometimes the mere threat of an initiative spurs the legislature into action that institutional gridlock might otherwise have prevented. In 2003 and 2004, after prodding by governors Davis and Schwarzenegger and the early signature-gathering efforts of an initiative proposal, the legislature reformed the state's workers' compensation program.[19] Conversely, the legislature's work on climate change was nearly undone in November 2010 by a business-sponsored initiative to delay implementation of AB 32. On this occasion, the voters elected to let the controversial law remain in place.

UNFINISHED BUSINESS

Today's legislature faces myriad issues, ranging from a questionable public education system to a deteriorating infrastructure. Faced with revolving participants, the legislature operates with little stability and less tradition. Term limits, restrictions on budget growth (see Chapter 8), and recession for most of the last decade have added to the woes of this policymaking body. Nothing has suffered more than the annual budget, which more times than not emerges well after the start of the next fiscal year. As a result, this outcome can be painful to recipients of services and programs, many of whom are poor, elderly, and sick.

In 2010, the voters attempted to ease budget gridlock by passing a ballot measure which reduced the required budget vote to a simple majority. But with an absolute two-thirds vote still required for raising revenues, it remains to be seen whether the change is anything but symbolic. Earlier, Governor Schwarzenegger tapped into voter anger when he casually suggested that the state would be better off with a part-time legislature, but he dropped the proposal after it garnered little traction in state public opinion polls. His contempt for the legislature seemed rather transparent, although Schwarzenegger isn't the only California to bear such sentiments.

Still, while the voters have blamed the legislature for gridlock, they rejected a ballot measure in 2010 that would have made it easier to pass budgets by reducing the required majority from two-thirds to a majority. Arnold Schwarzenegger tapped into this anger early on in his governorship when he casually suggested one day that perhaps the state would be better off with a part-time legislature, but he dropped the proposal after it garnered little traction in state public opinion polls. Yet his contempt for the legislature seems rather transparent, although he's not the only California governor ever to have borne such sentiments.

With all these pressures, legislators often seem to react to problems rather than to anticipate or solve them. As a consequence, public policies are made increasingly by initiative, the governor, or the courts. Nevertheless, the legislature continues to grapple with the leading issues of the day, and at least sometimes, lawmakers manage to overcome assorted obstacles in a fractured political environment to enact policies of substance.

NOTES

1. *Californians and Their Government*, Public Policy Institute of California Statewide Survey (San Francisco: PPIC, January 2010).

2. In general, the plan provided one senator per county. In a few cases, two low-populated counties shared a senator, and in one case, three low-populated counties—Alpine, Inyo, and Mono—shared a senator.

3. Legislators receive monthly allowances for cars (including gasoline and maintenance); life, health, dental, vision, and disability insurance; and a daily housing allowance when they are in session in Sacramento. On average these benefits amount to about $42,000 annually, almost all of which is nontaxable. For an interesting critique, see Dan Walters, "Legislative Per Diem Boondoggle," *Sacramento Bee*, July 7, 2007, p. A3.

4. The other full-time legislatures are Alaska, Florida, Massachusetts, Michigan, New Jersey, New York, Ohio, Pennsylvania, and Wisconsin.

5. "Plan to Redraw Districts Passes," *Los Angeles Times*, September 14, 2001, p. B8.

6. *Ibid*.

7. Rene Bukovichik Van Vechten, "Taking the Politics Out of Politics? State Legislative Politics and Institutional Reform in Twentieth Century California" (Ph.D. diss., University of California, Irvine 2002), 203–213.

8. *Ibid*, p. 21.

9. "Report Chronicles Downside of Term Limits," Stateline.org, August 16, 2006, www.stateline.org/live/details/story?contentId=134247.

10. Public Policy Institute of California, *Californians and Their Government*," (San Francisco: PPIC, September 10, 2009), p. 7.

11. Kathleen Les, "Mr. Mayor Goes to the Capitol," *California Journal* 30, no. 10 (October 1999): 36–38.

12. See Bruce E. Cain and That Kousser, *Adapting to Term Limits: Recent Experiences and New Directions* (San Francisco: Public Policy Institute of California, 2004), p. 15.

13. "Choosing Sides in State Budget Fiasco," *Los Angeles Times*, June 26, 2010, pp. A1, A14.

14. *Ibid*.

15. See "Ghost Voting: A Long History," *San Francisco Chronicle*, June 10, 2008, pp. A1, A16.

16. "What Limits? New Law Can't Stop Big Money," *Los Angeles Times*, September 3, 2003, pp. A1, A18.

17. Institute on Money and State Politics, "State Elections Overview, 2008," Helena, Mont., April 2010, www.followthemoney.org/database/StateGlance/state_candidates.phtml?s=CA&y=2008&f=0&so=a&p=7#sorttable (accessed April 2010).

18. "Dems Reject Two of Schwarzenegger's Parole Appointees," *Sacramento Bee*, June 26, 2008, p. A3.

19. "State Fund Posts 9.9% Dip in Comp Rates," *Los Angeles Times*, June 5, 2004, pp. C1, C2.

LEARN MORE ON THE WEB

California State Assembly:
www.assembly.ca.gov

California State Senate:
www.senate.ca.gov

Campaign finance:
www.followthemoney.org

Daily politics and policy-related news:
www.rtumble.com

Legislative Analyst's Office:
www.lao.ca.gov

Legislative histories and bill analyses:
  www.leginfo.ca.gov/bilinfo.html

National Conference of State Legislatures:
  www.ncsl.org

Search for your legislator:
  www.legislature.ca.gov/legislators_and_districts/districts/districts.html

Watch or listen to the legislature in session:
  www.legislature.ca.gov/the_state_legislature/calendar_and_schedules/
    audio_tv.html

LEARN MORE AT THE LIBRARY

Bill Boyarsky. *Big Daddy: Jesse Unruh and the Art of Power Politics.* Berkeley: University of California Press, 2008.

Willie L. Brown, Jr., and P. J. Corkery. *Basic Brown: My Life and Our Times.* New York: Simon & Schuster, 2008.

Gerald C. Lubenow, ed. *Governing California*, 2d ed. Berkeley, Calif.: Institute of Governmental Studies Press, 2006.

Gary F. Moncrief, Peverill Squire, and Malcolm Jewel. *Who Runs for the Legislature?* Upper Saddle River, N.J.: Prentice Hall, 2001.

Peter Schrag. *California: America's High Stakes Experiment.* Berkeley: University of California Press, 2006.

6

California Law: Courts, Judges, and Politics

CHAPTER CONTENTS

Courts are very much a part of the political process. Judges and politicians have always known this, but the public has been slower to understand the political nature of the judiciary. When governors made controversial appointments to the courts during the 1970s and 1980s, however, judicial politics became a very public matter. Later, judicial politics became apparent in court decisions that overturned popular initiatives and, of course, in the appointment and confirmation of justices to the United States Supreme Court.

What makes the courts political? It's not just controversial judicial decisions or even the involvement of party politicians. Courts are political because their judgments are choices between public policy alternatives. When judges consider cases, they evaluate the issues before them both in terms of existing legislation and in the context of the U.S. and California constitutions. Rulings based on differing judicial interpretations of these documents help some people and hurt others. This is why the courts, like members of the executive and legislative branches, are subject to the attentions and pressures of California's competing interests, and this is why the courts are political.

THE CALIFORNIA COURT SYSTEM

The California court system is the largest in the nation, with more than two thousand judicial officers and nineteen thousand court employees. The three levels within the system are linked, but each has its own responsibilities. Most cases begin and end at the lowest level. Only a few move up the state's judicial ladder through the appeals process (see Figure 6.1), and even fewer end up in the United States Supreme Court.

The Judicial Ladder

The vast majority of cases begin and end in trial courts, the bottom rung of the judicial ladder. In California, **superior courts** in each county are the trial courts, handling misdemeanor cases (minor crimes, including most traffic offenses), felonies (serious crimes subject to sentences of one year or more in state prison), civil suits (noncriminal disputes), divorces, and juvenile cases. Superior courts also operate small claims courts, where individuals can take cases with damage claims up to $7,500 before a judge without attorneys—sort of like television's *Judge Judy*.

Losers in trial courts may ask the court on the next rung of the judicial ladder to review the decision. Most cases aren't appealed, but when major crimes and penalties or big money are involved, the losers in the cases sometimes request a review by one of California's six district **courts of appeal**. As appellate bodies, these courts do not hold trials like the ones we see on television. Lawyers make arguments and submit briefs to panels of three justices, who try to determine whether the original trial was conducted fairly. These justices consider only possible legal errors, not the verdict in the case. If they find errors, they can send the case back for another trial or even dismiss the charges.

Ultimately, parties to the cases may petition for review by the seven-member state **supreme court**, the top of California's judicial ladder. Few cases reach this level because most are resolved in the lower courts and the high court declines most of the petitions. When the California Supreme Court hears a case, its decision is final unless issues of federal law or the U.S. Constitution arise; the United States Supreme Court may consider such cases.

If a higher court refuses an appeal, the lower court's decision stands. Even when a case is accepted, the justices of the higher court have agreed only to consider the issues. They may or may not overturn the decision of the lower court.

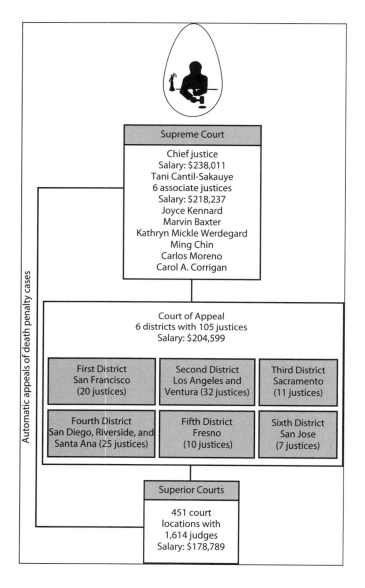

FIGURE 6.1 The California Court System

SOURCE: California Judicial Council

Judicial Election and Selection

Although the tiered structure of the California courts is similar to that of the federal courts, the selection of judges is not. Federal judges and members of the United States Supreme Court are appointed by the president subject to confirmation by the U.S. Senate. Once appointed, they serve for life. California judges and justices, however, gain office through a more complicated process and regularly face the voters. This periodic scrutiny by the public, the media, and interest groups helps keep judges and their decisions in the news.

Formal qualifications to become a judge are few: candidates must have been admitted to practice law in California for at least ten years. Technically, superior court judges are elected, but most actually gain office through appointment by the governor when a sitting judge dies, retires, or is promoted between elections. The governor also appoints people to the bench when the legislature creates new judgeships. A governor who is elected to two terms of office may appoint as many as half of the state's sitting judges, significantly affecting judicial practices. Governors generally appoint judges who are members of their own political parties, although Republican governor Arnold Schwarzenegger was more willing than any of his predecessors to appoint judges who are not members of his own political party.[1] Prior service as a district attorney (prosecutor) is common for successful appointees—a fact leading to complaints that judges in general are biased against defendants and defense attorneys.[2]

Appointed judges must run for office when their terms expire, but running as incumbents, they almost always win. Superior court judges can also gain office simply by declaring their candidacy for a specific judicial office and then running. If no candidate wins a majority in the primary election, the two candidates with the most votes face each other in a **runoff election** in November. Superior court judges serve six-year terms and then may run for reelection, usually without opposition. Judges have no term limits.

Appointments and the Higher Courts

Unlike lower court judges, members of the district courts of appeal and the state supreme court attain office only by gubernatorial appointment. The governor's possible nominees are first screened by the state's legal community through its Commission on Judicial Nominees Evaluation. Then the nominees must be approved by the **Commission on Judicial Appointments**, consisting of the attorney general, the chief justice of the state supreme court, and the senior presiding justice of the courts of appeal. The commission may reject a nominee, but it has done so only twice since its creation in 1934.

Once approved by the Commission on Judicial Appointments, the new justices take office, but they must go before the voters at the next gubernatorial election. No opponents or political party labels appear on the ballot; the voters simply check yes or no on the retention of the justices in question. If approved, they serve the remainder of the twelve-year term of the person they have replaced, at which time they can seek voter confirmation for a standard twelve-year term and additional terms after that.

Eleven other states select their supreme court justices in a similar fashion, but twenty-six rely solely on elections. The governor or legislature appoints justices in the remaining twelve states.

Firing Judges

Almost all judges easily win election and reelection, mostly without opposition. Those who designed the system probably intended it to be this way. They wanted to distance judges somewhat from politics and to ensure their independence by giving them relatively long terms, thus also ensuring relatively consistent interpretation of the law. Avoiding costly election campaigns that depend on financial contributors also promotes independence. The framers of the U.S. Constitution put such a high value on judicial continuity and independence that they provided for selection by appointment rather than by election and allowed judges to serve for life. For most of California's history, these values also seemed well entrenched in the political culture, and the state's judges functioned without much criticism or interference. Nevertheless, California's constitution provides several mechanisms of judicial accountability, all of which have been used recently. Judges can be removed through elections, but they can also be reprimanded or removed by the judicial system itself.

Incumbent justices of the California Supreme Court routinely won reelection without serious challenge until 1966, when a backlash against decisions that supported racial integration led to an unsuccessful campaign to unseat justices who were viewed as too liberal. Over the next two decades, several lower court judges faced challenges because critics viewed them as lenient toward criminals, and some were defeated. Although early efforts to oust liberal members of the state supreme court failed, anticourt elements triumphed in 1986, when Chief Justice Rose Bird and two other liberal justices appointed by former Democratic governor Jerry Brown were swept out of office—the only justices removed by the voters in California history. Since then, the anticourt fervor has subsided. Today, sitting judges are rarely challenged.

Judges also can be removed by the judicial system itself. The **Commission on Judicial Performance** was created in 1960 to investigate charges of misconduct or incompetence. Its members include three judges (appointed by the supreme court), two lawyers (appointed by the governor), and six public members (two each appointed by the governor, the senate Rules Committee, and the speaker of the assembly). Few investigations result in any action, but if the charges are confirmed, the commission may impose censure, removal from office, or forced retirement.

Hundreds of complaints against judges are filed with the commission each year; about one-third are investigated. In the rare cases in which the commission finds a judge to be at fault, it usually issues a warning or reprimand. Even more rarely, the commission may remove a judge from the bench. In recent years, judges have been removed for lying about campaign funds, threatening a district attorney, inappropriate interventions in trials, and in one case, excessive delays and neglect of court orders. Actual removals from the bench are rare, however, because those whose conduct is questionable usually resign before the commission's investigation is completed.

THE COURTS AT WORK

In 2007–2008, 9,552,781 cases were filed in California's trial courts. Traffic infractions made up 68.4 percent of these cases. Felony and misdemeanor (criminal) cases numbered 1,252,556 (13.1 percent), and the balance were civil suits (on contract disputes, for example) or divorce and family law cases.[3]

California's constitution guarantees the right to a jury trial for both criminal and civil cases; if both parties agree, however, a judge alone may hear the case. In jury trials, prospective jurors are drawn from lists of licensed drivers, voters, and property owners, but finding a twelve-member jury is often difficult. Many people avoid jury duty because it takes time away from work and pays only a few dollars a day. Homemakers and retired people are most readily available, but they alone cannot make up a balanced jury. Poor people and minorities tend to be underrepresented because they are less likely to be on the lists from which jurors are drawn and because some avoid participation in a system that they distrust.

The parties in civil cases provide their own lawyers, although legal aid societies sometimes help those who can't afford counsel. In criminal cases, the **district attorney**, an elected county official, carries out the prosecution. Defendants hire their own attorney or are provided with a court-appointed attorney if they cannot afford one. California's larger counties employ a **public defender** to provide such assistance. Well over half of all felony defendants require court-appointed help.

Most cases never go to trial, though. In over 90 percent of all criminal cases, the defendant pleads guilty, often by **plea bargaining**, which results in a pretrial agreement on a plea and a penalty. Plea bargaining reduces the heavy workload of the courts and guarantees some punishment or restitution, but it also allows those charged with a crime to serve shorter sentences than they might have received if convicted of all charges. Most civil suits are also settled without a trial because the parties to the cases reach an agreement to avoid the high costs and long delays of a trial. Only about 0.1 percent of all cases are tried before a jury (11,218 in 2007–2008); a judge alone hears the others that go to trial.[4]

It is important to note that the judicial system as a whole—including judges, prosecutors, public defenders, lawyers, and juries—does not reflect the diversity of California's people. About 83 percent of California's nearly 170,000 active attorneys are non-Hispanic whites, even though minority group members make up 58 percent of the population. About one-third of the state's attorneys are women, however—a number that is quickly rising.[5] Ethnic representation among California's judges is similar: 71 percent are male, and 73 percent are white.[6] These numbers lead critics to express concern about the fact that a predominantly white judicial system metes out justice to defendants who are, in the majority, nonwhite and that punishment is less severe for whites than for minorities convicted of the same crime.[7] African Americans, and to a lesser extent other minorities, perceive this situation and express deep mistrust of the system. Minority participation as attorneys and court officials has increased over time (Table 6.1 shows increasing diversity in judicial appointments), but considerable disparities remain.

Appeals

When a dispute arises over a trial proceeding or its outcome, the losing party may appeal to a higher court to review the case. Most appeals are refused, but the higher courts may agree to hear a case because of previous procedural

TABLE 6.1 Judicial Appointments by California Governors, 1959–2010

	Male	Female	Non-Hispanic White	Non-Hispanic Black	Hispanic	Asian
Ronald Reagan (R), 1967–1975	97.4% (478)	2.6% (13)	93.1% (457)	2.6% (13)	3.3% (16)	1.0% (5)
Jerry Brown (D), 1975–1983	84.0 (691)	16.0 (132)	75.5 (621)	10.9 (90)	9.4 (77)	4.3 (35)
George Deukmejian (R), 1983–1991	84.8 (821)	15.2 (147)	87.7 (849)	3.6 (35)	5.0 (49)	3.6 (35)
Pete Wilson (R), 1991–1998	74.6 (517)	25.4 (176)	84.4 (585)	5.2 (36)	4.9 (34)	5.5 (38)
Gray Davis (D), 1999–2003	65.8 (237)	34.2 (123)	70.8 (255)	9.25 (33)	12.8 (46)	7.2 (26)
Arnold Schwarzenegger (R), 2003–2010	65.0 (370)	35.0 (199)	73.7 (419)	7.6 (43)	10.7 (61)	8.0 (46)

SOURCE: Governor's Office.

problems (for instance, if the defendant was not read his or her rights) or because it raises untested legal issues. Appellate courts do not retry the case or review the facts in evidence; their job is to determine whether the original trial was fair and the law was applied appropriately. In addition to traditional appellate cases, the state supreme court also automatically reviews all death penalty decisions. Although few in number (17 in 2007–2008), these cases take up a substantial amount of the supreme court's time. A few other cases come to it directly. Known as *original proceedings,* these include cases involving writs of *mandamus* (ordering a government action) and *habeas corpus* (a request for reasons why someone is in custody). Neither the courts of appeal nor the state supreme court can initiate cases. No matter how eager they are to intervene in an issue, they have to wait for someone else to bring the case to them.

Every year, about 10,000 petitions are filed with the California Supreme Court, mostly requesting reviews of cases decided by the courts of appeal. Each year the members of the court, meeting "in conference," choose about two hundred petitions for consideration, a task that consumes an estimated 40 percent of the court's time. By refusing to hear a case, the court allows the preceding decision to stand. When the court grants a hearing, one of the justices (or a staff member) writes a calendar memo analyzing the case. Attorneys representing the two sides present written briefs and then oral arguments, during which they face rigorous questioning by the justices.

After hearing the oral arguments, the justices discuss the case in conference and vote in order of seniority; the chief justice casts the final, and sometimes decisive, vote. If the chief justice agrees with the majority, he or she can assign a justice to write the official court opinion; usually this is the same justice who wrote the initial calendar memo. A draft of the opinion then circulates among the justices, each of whom may concur, suggest changes, or write a dissenting opinion. Finally, after many months, the court's decision is made public. The court issued 116 opinions in 2007–2008—about 1 percent of all the cases filed.

This time-consuming process allows plenty of room for politicking among the justices and depends on a high degree of cooperation and deferential behavior among them—what judges call **collegiality**—as a way of building consensus on issues under consideration. With seven independent minds on the court, ongoing negotiations are needed to reach a majority and a decision.

Running the Courts

In addition to deciding cases, the chief justice acts as the administrative head of the California court system. This entails setting procedures for hearings and deliberations, managing public information for the supreme court, and overseeing its staff. The chief justice also assigns cases to specific appellate courts and appoints temporary justices when there are vacancies on the supreme court due to disqualification, illness, or retirement.

As chair of the **Judicial Council,** the chief justice also takes a hand in managing the entire state court system. The Judicial Council has twenty-one members, including fourteen judges (appointed by the chief justice), four attorneys (appointed by the state bar association), and one member from each house of the state legislature. The Judicial Council makes the rules for court procedures, collects data on the operations and workload of the courts, and oversees the Administrative Office of the Courts with 901 employees and a $220 million budget. During the state budget crisis of 2009, the Judicial Council voted to close the courts one day a month, despite an increasing workload.

THE HIGH COURT AS A POLITICAL BATTLEGROUND

The courts are particularly important and powerful in California because of the nature of California's government and politics. California's constitution has been amended more than five hundred times since it was written in 1879, making it both long and elaborately specific, with components addressing all sorts of matters, both major and mundane. The density of California's constitution is reflected in the structures of government it sets out and is increased through constant revision by initiative. In turn, the length, detail, and continually changing complexity of California's constitution give the courts greater power, because they have the job of determining whether laws and public policy are consistent with the constitution. One scholar called the courts a "shadow government"[8] because of their importance in shaping public policy, but others view this as the courts' appropriate constitutional role.

At the top of California's judicial ladder is the state supreme court, the ultimate interpreter of the state constitution (unless issues arise under the U.S.

Constitution). The court's power makes it a center of political interest: governors strive to appoint justices who share their values and pay close attention to the appointment process. As governors have changed, so have the sorts of justices they appoint. And as its membership has changed, the California Supreme Court has moved across the spectrum from liberal to conservative.

Regardless of its collective political values, the court has not backed away from tackling controversial issues, including occasionally overturning decisions of the legislature or the people (as expressed in initiatives). This willingness is less because of interventionist attitudes on the part of the justices than because of a long, complex, and frequently amended constitution and poorly written laws and initiatives.

Governors, Voters, and the Courts

Long dominated by liberals, California's supreme court took a distinct turn toward the right in 1986, after the voters rejected the reelections of three liberal justices, including Rose Bird, the controversial chief justice at the time. Appointed in 1977 by Governor Jerry Brown, Bird and her colleagues waded into controversy with unpopular rulings on busing for school desegregation and Proposition 13 (the popular property tax reduction initiative), as well as consistently reversing death sentences even as public concern about crime increased. When Bird and two other liberal justices were on the ballot in 1986, conservative Republican governor George Deukmejian led a successful campaign to defeat them. With three new openings, Deukmejian transformed the court with conservative appointees, including a new chief justice.

Subsequent appointees have maintained the court's conservative majority. Today's court includes Marvin Baxter and Joyce Kennard (both Deukmejian appointees) and Kathryn Werdegar and Ming Chin (appointed by Republican governor Pete Wilson). Governor Gray Davis appointed Carlos Moreno, the court's only Democrat, in 2001. The newest justices are Carol A. Corrigan, a 2006 appointment by Governor Schwarzenegger, and Tani Cantil-Sakauye, appointed chief justice by Schwarzenegger in 2010. Minority members of the court include Cantil-Sakauye (who is Filipina), Moreno (who is Latino), Chin (who is Chinese), and Kennard (who is Dutch-Indonesian). Four of the court's seven members are women. All of the current justices have won voter approval, with 65 to 76 percent voting for their retention. Cantil-Sakauye was confirmed for a 12-year term by the voters in 2010 and Justices Chin and Moreno each won an additional 12-year term that year.

With a majority of the justices appointed by Republican governors and solidly confirmed by the voters, California's supreme court today is moderately conservative and less controversial than in the past. The court's conservatism is reflected in its tendency to be pro-prosecution in criminal cases and pro-business in economic cases.[9] The court also disappointed local governments seeking new taxes with rulings that rigidly applied a requirement for two-thirds voter approval, a strict interpretation of 1978's Proposition 13 (see Chapter 8).

Overall, the supreme court avoids **judicial activism** (making policy through court decisions rather than through the legislative or electoral process), but even the current conservative court sometimes asserts its independence, wading into political controversy and significantly affecting state politics. For example, it has followed the Bird court's precedent of approving state-funded abortions, and in 1997 the court ruled against Governor Pete Wilson's plan to privatize the work of the state transportation agency. In 2009, the court rejected a plan by the governor and state legislature to solve their own budget problems by taking transportation and redevelopment funds from local governments.

Most controversially, the courts sometimes overrule decisions of the voters, as they did when they struck down portions of voter-approved initiatives that required tougher sentences of criminals because the proposals shifted discretion from judges to prosecutors. Probably the highest-profile and most controversial action taken by the supreme court, however, was its 2008 ruling on same-sex marriage. When the City and County of San Francisco licensed such marriages in 2004, the supreme court ruled the marriages illegal on the basis of state law, as approved by the voters in 2002. But the constitutionality of that law was challenged in 2008, and on a four-to-three vote, the court ruled that "the California Constitution properly must be interpreted to guarantee this basic civil right to all Californians, whether gay or heterosexual, and to same-sex couples as well as to opposite-sex couples."[10] Opponents quickly qualified **Proposition 8**, an initiative constitutional amendment to restrict marriage to opposite-sex couples. Voters approved the measure, thus overruling the court. That initiative was subsequently challenged in court, but the California Supreme Court accepted it as a legitimate amendment to the state constitution. Then chief justice George wrote that the court's decision was not based on whether Proposition 8 "is wise or sound as a matter of policy," but rather "concerns the right of the people . . . to change or alter the state constitution itself . . . Regardless of our views as individuals on this question of policy, we recognize as judges and as a court our responsibility to confine our consideration to a determination of the constitutional validity and legal effect of the measure in question."[11]

This decision did not put the issue to rest, however. The federal courts are sometimes drawn into battles over California initiatives, too. Since the 1990s, federal courts have overturned initiatives on campaign finance, open primary elections, and limits on public services for immigrants as violations of the U.S. Constitution, which trumps any state law or state constitution. In 2010, proponents of same-sex marriage took their case to a federal district court, arguing that Proposition 8 constituted a denial of equal rights under the U.S. Constitution. The judge in that case ruled in favor of the plaintiffs, thus overriding both the voters of the state of California and the state supreme court. The federal court ruling is being appealed, and the final decision will rest with the United States Supreme Court—or the voters of California when the issue comes back to them in yet another initiative.

Although judicial rulings against voter-approved laws appear undemocratic, the state and federal courts are doing their duty by interpreting these controversial propositions not only for their content but also for their consistency with the California and U.S. constitutions. When the courts find an act of another branch of government or of the voters to be contrary to existing law or to the state or federal constitution, it is their responsibility to overturn that law, even if their decision is unpopular. "When we invalidate one of these initiatives," former chief justice George argued, "what we are doing is not thwarting the public's will. We are adhering to the ultimate expression of the popular will: the Constitution of the United States, or the Constitution of the State of California, which has been adopted by the people and which imposes limits on the initiative process and on lawmaking by legislatures and by the executive."[12]

As controversial as the California Supreme Court's decisions sometimes are, the court's influence goes well beyond this state. A study of court decisions throughout the country found that courts in other states followed precedents set in California more than precedents set in the courts of any other state.[13] This suggests that the California court is well within the mainstream of jurisprudence in the United States. It's also one reason why the court battle over same-sex marriages was so hard fought.

COURTS AND THE POLITICS OF CRIME

Crime topped the list of voter concerns in California and the nation during much of the 1980s and 1990s. Murder, rape, burglary, gang wars, and random violence seemed all too common. Republicans George Deukmejian and Pete Wilson were elected governor at least partly because they were seen as law-and-order candidates.

Capital punishment was a key issue in the 1980s, when a liberal supreme court overturned the vast majority of the death penalty cases it reviewed. Since 1986, when the voters rejected these liberals, the supreme court has affirmed most death sentences. The issue has not gone away, however. Law-and-order advocates still condemn the lengthy delays that plague death penalty appeals—up to ten years for the state courts and another ten years for the federal courts—but experts say that much of the delay is because the courts are unable to either find legal counsel for the condemned or handle the workload. A recent report called the system "broken" and "dysfunctional."[14] Neither the proponents nor the opponents of the death penalty are satisfied with its current administration. Meanwhile, forensic methods such as DNA testing have revealed wrongful convictions in death penalty cases so frequently that a moratorium on executions has been proposed.

In 2006 a federal judge took the issue of capital punishment out of the state courts with a ruling suspending executions in California due to concerns about the drugs used for lethal injections and the conditions of outdated prison facilities for executions. Since then, the state has built a new death chamber, but executions remained suspended as of 2010 because the state failed to satisfy the federal court regarding lethal injections.

Law-and-order proponents also pushed for tougher sentences for other crimes. Beginning in the 1980s, voters passed a series of initiatives that strengthened penalties for many crimes, and in 1994 the electorate approved the "three-strikes" initiative. The new law reflected the view that liberal judges who were "soft on crime" were letting criminals off with light sentences. **"Three strikes"** required anyone convicted of three felonies to serve a sentence of twenty-five years to life: "three strikes and you're out."

The three-strikes law quickly increased the state's prison population, as well as its spending on prisons (see Chapter 8). New prisons were built, and operating the state prison system absorbs an ever-growing share of the state budget. With many of the state's worst criminals incarcerated for life, three-strikes prosecutions declined, and so did California's crime rate. Violent crime in California peaked in 1992 (two years before the three-strikes law) and has declined since then. In 2008 the number of violent crimes was about the same as in 1979, even with 14 million more people living in the state.[15] Conservatives attribute this decline to tougher judges and penalties, but many experts argue that the declining crime rate was due to economic prosperity and demographics, with fewer people in the age group that is most commonly associated with criminal activity. Even in the recent recession, crime rates continue to decline. In any case, crime has resonated far less as an issue in recent statewide elections. In the last few years, education, the economy, and health care have outranked crime as the top concerns of California voters.

Meanwhile, the prison population in California remains huge, which means the cost of incarcerating all these men and women is also huge. But despite a massive investment of tax funds, California's prisons are overcrowded and beset by violence and disease. A system built for 84,271 inmates housed 173,479 in 2006 (a historic high) and 168,830 in 2009.[16] Conditions in the prison health-care system were so bad that a class action suit was brought to a federal court, which intervened on grounds that these conditions constituted "cruel and unusual punishment" under the U.S. Constitution. In 2005 a federal judge put the prison health system in the hands of a court-appointed monitor. In 2009, seeing minimal progress, federal judges gave the state forty-five days to come up with a plan to reduce the prison population—and then rejected the plan submitted by Governor Schwarzenegger, who was unable to persuade the legislature to fund new prisons or approve release of some prisoners (the elderly or low-level offenders, for example). Schwarzenegger appealed the case to the United States Supreme Court, but a ruling was not expected before 2011.

CALIFORNIA LAW

Crime and other issues discussed in this chapter remind us that the courts play a central role in the politics of our state. Controversies about judicial appointments and decisions make the political nature of the courts apparent, especially when the rulings of the court conflict with the will of the electorate as expressed in initiatives. Yet the courts can never be free of politics. They make policy and interpret the law, and their judgments vary with the values of those who make them.

NOTES

1. "Forum Sheds Light on How Judges Are Screened, Chosen," *San Jose Mercury News,* June 4, 2006. As of 2006, 54 percent of Schwarzenegger's appointees were Republican, 34 percent were Democrats, and 12 percent had "unstated" party affiliations.

2. Rodney F. Kingsnorth, "Change How We Appoint Judges," in *Remaking California,* ed. R. Jeffrey Lustig (Berkeley, Calif.: Heyday Books, 2010), pp. 226–227.

3. Judicial Council, *2009 Court Statistics Report,* www.courtinfo.ca.gov (accessed July 7, 2010).

4. *Ibid.*

5. California Bar Association, "The State Bar of California: What Does It Do? How Does It Work?" 2006, www.calbar.org (accessed August 12, 2008).

6. Judicial Council of California, "Demographic Data Provided by Justices and Judges Relative to Gender and Race/Ethnicity," www.courtinfo.ca.gov (accessed July 7, 2010).

7. Elsa Y. Chen, "Cumulative Disadvantage and Racial and Ethnic Disparities in California Federal Sentencing," in *Racial and Ethnic Politics in California,* ed. Sandra Bass and Bruce M. Cain (Berkeley: Public Policy Press, Institute of Governmental Studies, University of California, 2008).

8. Charles Price, "Shadow Government," *California Journal,* October 1997, p. 38.

9. See Preble Stolz, Gerald F. Uelmen, and Susan Rasky, "The California Supreme Court," in *Governing California,* ed. Gerald C. Lubenow, 2d ed. (Berkeley: Public Policy Press, Institute of Governmental Studies, University of California, 2006), p. 103.

10. *In re Marriage Cases,* S147999.

11. *Strauss v. Horton,* S168047; *Tyler v. State of California,* S168066; and *City and County of San Francisco v. Horton,* S168078, www.courtinfo.ca.gov/courts/supreme.

12. Ronald George, "Promoting Judicial Independence," *The Commonwealth,* February 2006, p. 10.

13. Jake Dear and Edward W. Jesson, "Followed Rates and Leading Cases, 1940–2005," *University of California, Davis, Law Review* 41 (April 2007): 683.

14. California Commission on the Fair Administration of Justice, "Fair Administration of the Death Penalty," June 30, 2008, www.ccfaj.org (accessed August 1, 2008).

15. "California Crime Rates, 1960-2008," www.disastercenter.com/crime/cacrime.htm (accessed July 9, 2010).

16. Department of Corrections, "Population Reports," www.cdcr.ca.gov (accessed July 9, 2010).

LEARN MORE ON THE WEB

California's court system:
www.courtinfo.ca.gov

California Court Association:
www.calcourt.org

For more on the courts:
    www.judgepedia.org

State Bar of California:
    www.calbar.org

Ratings of attorneys:
    www.avvo.com

LEARN MORE AT THE LIBRARY

Elsa Y. Chen. " Cumulative Disadvantage and Racial and Ethnic Disparities in California Federal Sentencing." In *Racial and Ethnic Politics in California*, edited by Sandra Bass and Bruce M. Cain. Berkeley: Berkeley Public Policy Press, Institute of Governmental Studies, University of California, 2008.

Preble Stolz, Gerald F. Uelmen, and Susan Rasky. " The California Supreme Court." In *Governing California*, 2d ed., edited by Gerald C. Lubenow. Berkeley: Berkeley Public Policy Press, Institute of Governmental Studies, University of California, 2006.

Franklin E. Zimring, Sam Kamin, and Gordon Hawkins. *Crime and Punishment in California: The Impact of Three Strikes and You're Out.* Berkeley, Calif: Institute of Governmental Studies Press, 1999.

7

The Executive Branch: Coping with Fragmented Authority

CHAPTER CONTENTS

The **governor** is California's most powerful public official. He or she shapes the state budget, appoints key policymakers in the executive and judicial branches, and both responds to and shapes public opinion by taking positions on controversial issues. The governor also is the state's chief administrator; the unofficial leader of his or her political party; and liaison to other states, the U.S. government, and other nations. There are times when the governor's powers extend even beyond their normally broad limits to international issues such as immigration or global warming. At times, the governor's performance can generate intense reactions, as evidenced by the public's rejection of the items put forth in special elections by Governor Arnold Schwarzenegger in 2005 and 2009. No one in state government is in the spotlight as often the governor.

Unlike the president of the United States, the governor of California shares authority with seven other independently elected executive officers. Occasionally, these other executives clash with the governor over the use of power, as do the legislature and the judiciary. Simply put, the executive branch is anything but a unified body. Endless schisms between officeholders contribute to the state's fragmentation.

There has been one change in the drama among elected officials, however. Term limits, although applicable to both the executive and legislative branches, have left the governor in a stronger position relative to the legislature because of the governor's near certainty of two 4-year terms of office. With legislative leaders ascending to power on much shorter time schedules, the governor's experience has worked to his favor.

THE GOVERNOR: FIRST AMONG EQUALS

The current governor of California, Democrat Edmund J. ("Jerry") Brown, Jr., was elected in 2010. Brown succeeded Arnold Schwarzenegger, who had been elected after the recall of Gray Davis from office (see Table 7.1). With an annual salary of $206,500, he is the highest-paid chief executive of the fifty states. The governor of New York, second highest in the nation, receives $179,000. Still, this compensation is well below the salaries earned by many other government employees in California, particularly in large cities and counties. Even among state employees, prison wardens, retirement program coordinators, physicians, and university presidents earn considerably more than the governor.

T A B L E 7.1 California Governors and Their Parties, 1943–2015

Name	Party	Dates in Office
Earl Warren	Republican[*]	1943–1953
Goodwin J. Knight	Republican	1953–1959
Edmund G. Brown, Sr.	Democrat	1959–1967
Ronald Reagan	Republican	1967–1975
Jerry Brown	Democrat	1975–1983
George Deukmejian	Republican	1983–1991
Pete Wilson	Republican	1991–1999
Gray Davis	Democrat	1999–November 2003
Arnold Schwarzenegger	Republican	2003–2011
Jerry Brown	Democrat	2011–2015

*Warren cross-filed as both a Republican and a Democrat in 1946 and 1950.

SOURCE: California Secretary of State.

Jerry Brown's election to the governor's office is the latest example of California's bizarre politics. A political fixture in the state since his first election to the Los Angeles Community College District Board of Trustees in 1969 (that's not a typo!), Brown served was elected governor in 1974 and 1978 after serving as the Secretary of State. His father, Edmund G. (Pat) Brown also was governor in 1958 and 1962. Because his governorship occurred before California adopted term limits in 1990, Brown was eligible to run again. With his third term Brown is in rare company. Only Earl Warren was elected to three terms in the pre-term limit era.

Brown's election is significant on another way: He was outspent by a margin of more than 6-to-1, courtesy of Meg Whitman's largely self-funded campaign in which the Republican donated $175 million of her own fund to her ill-fated cause. Indeed, a cornerstone of Brown's campaign accused Whitman of trying to buy the governorship. Apparently there was no sale.

Formal Powers

Much of the governor's authority comes from formal powers written into the state's constitution and its laws. These responsibilities guide his or her relationships with the legislative and judicial branches, as well as with the other office-holders in the executive branch.

Submission of an Annual Budget   No formal power is more important than the governor's budgetary responsibilities. The budget outlines the sources of state revenues and the programmatic recipients of state funds. According to the state constitution, the governor must recommend a balanced budget to the legislature within the first ten days of each calendar year. Budget work is virtually a year-round task, and it consumes more of the governor's time than just about any other activity except responding to emergencies such as earthquakes or fires. The governor is assisted in this effort by an appointed **director of finance**, the key person in charge of developing the budget document, who spends months with his or her staff gathering data and budget requests from the dozens of departments and agencies that make up the state's bureaucracy. Initial preparations begin on July 1—the start of the fiscal year—and culminate with the governor's submission of a proposal to the legislature the following January (see Chapter 8). Officially, the annual process ends with the signing of the budget document by the governor before the end of the fiscal on June 30, so that the next year can begin with a budget in place. More often than not, however, budget negotiations linger well into summer.

Vetoes   The state constitution requires the legislature to respond to the governor's budget no later than June 15 so that the budget can go into effect by July 1—a formidable task because the proposed document is several hundred pages in length. Technically, legislators can disregard any or all parts of the budget package and pass their own version, but usually they stay reasonably close to the governor's proposals. They realize that the governor has the final say, albeit with some limitations. The governor cannot add money, but he or she can reduce or eliminate expenditures through use of the **item veto** before signing the budget into law. An absolute two-thirds vote from each house of the legislature—a near impossibility (see Chapter 5)—is necessary to overturn item vetoes. Accordingly, legislators often attempt to head off vetoes by negotiating with the governor in advance.

Of course, bills on topics other than budget matters also reach the governor's desk. Whereas the item veto is restricted to appropriations measures, the **general veto** allows the governor to reject any other bill passed by the legislature. It, too, can be overturned only by an absolute two-thirds vote in each house. Over a period of more than twenty years, George Deukmejian, Pete Wilson, and Gray Davis exercised general and item vetoes without a single one being overturned by the legislature.

Arnold Schwarzenegger used the veto even more than Davis, wielding his veto pen with vigor (see Table 7.2). He vetoed more than one-fourth of the bills that reached his desk. More than any governor in history, Schwarzenegger turned the veto into a potent legislative weapon. And, as with his immediate predecessors, he did not suffer any legislative rejections.

Under most circumstances, the governor has twelve days to act after the legislature passes a bill. On the hundreds of bills enacted by the legislature at a session's end, however, the governor has thirty days to act. Only a veto can keep a bill from becoming law. After the governor's time limit has passed, any unsigned or unvetoed bill becomes law the following January (unless the bill is an urgency measure, in which case it takes effect immediately upon signature).

Special Session. If the governor believes that the legislature has not addressed an important issue, he or she can take the dramatic step of calling a **special session**. At that time, the lawmakers must discuss only the specific business proposed by the governor. Special sessions often are called to respond to specific crises, as when Governor Schwarzenegger called on the legislature in 2006 to correct a prison system so overcrowded that a federal judge assumed oversight responsibilities.[1] He also called special sessions on health-care reform, water

TABLE 7.2 Vetoes and Overrides, 1967–2010

Governor	Bills Vetoed (%)	Vetoes Overridden
Ronald Reagan (1967–1975)	7.3	1
Jerry Brown (1975–1983)	6.3	13
George Deukmejian (1983–1991)	15.1	0
Pete Wilson (1991–1999)	16.6	0
Gray Davis (1999–November 2003)	17.6	0
Arnold Schwarzenegger (November 2003–2011)	26.4	0

SOURCE: Clerk, California State Senate.

policy, public education, and repeatedly on state budget deficits. Schwarzenegger called sixteen special sessions during his years in office—the most of any governor in state history—leading some to believe that he had diluted the significance of the concept.[2]

Executive Order.   On occasion, the governor can make policy by signing an **executive order**, an action that looks similar to legislation. Governors must exercise this power carefully because such moves often lead to lawsuits over the breadth of their powers. Immediately after taking office in 2003, Arnold Schwarzenegger signed an executive order to repeal the vehicle license fee, a revenue source that had been restored by Governor Gray Davis to reduce the state deficit but that offended many voters. By taking this action, Schwarzenegger honored a crucial campaign promise, although removal of the motor vehicle license fee contributed to a revenue gap almost as large as the one that helped chase Gray Davis from office. Later in his tenure, Schwarzenegger used the executive order to force furloughs on state workers as a means of lessening the state's budget deficit. Here he was only partially successful, as lawsuits overturned the furloughs affecting about one-fourth of the state's workers.[3]

Appointment Powers.   The governor's appointment powers, although substantial, are somewhat more restricted than his or her budgetary authority because others must approve all appointments except personal staff. Moreover, gubernatorial appointees hold only the top policymaking positions in the state system. Before the Progressive reforms, California governors could rely on patronage, or the "spoils" system, to hire friends and political allies. Today, 99 percent of all state employees are not appointed by the governor but rather are selected through a civil service system based on merit. The governor still fills about 2,500 key positions in the executive departments and cabinet agencies, except for the Departments of Justice and Education, whose heads are elected by the public. Together, these appointees direct the state bureaucracy (see Figure 7.1).

The state senate must approve most of the governor's appointees. Generally, senate confirmation is routine, but occasionally the governor's choice for a key post is rejected for reasons other than qualifications. In instances of an opening in the executive branch, both houses must weigh in with positive majorities. In early 2010, the legislature confirmed the selection of Abel Maldonado to fill the lieutenant governor vacancy that resulted from Lieutenant Governor John Garamendi's winning election to a vacated seat in the House of Representatives. After several months of fits and starts, Maldonado was confirmed and ran as the incumbent in the November 2010 general election.

The governor also appoints people to more than three hundred state boards and commissions. Membership on some boards—such as the Arts Council and the Commission on Aging, which have only advisory authority—is largely ceremonial and without pay. Other boards, however, such as the California Energy Commission (CEC), the Public Utilities Commission (PUC), the California Coastal Commission (CCC), and the California Division of Occupational Safety and Health (DOSH; better known as Cal-OSHA), make important policies free from gubernatorial control. Nevertheless, the governor affects key "independent" boards through his or her appointments and manipulation of the budget.

Perhaps the most enduring of all gubernatorial appointments are judgeships. The governor fills both vacancies and new judgeships that are periodically created by the legislature. In his eight years as governor, Pete Wilson filled 693 posts. During his five years in office, Gray Davis appointed 360 judges. Between his election in 2003 and 2010, Arnold Schwarzenegger appointed 545 judges, including two members of the state supreme court. Most judges continue to serve long after those who appointed them have gone. However, the governor's power is checked here to a degree, too, by various judicial commissions and by the voters in future elections. During his tenure as governor, Arnold Schwarzenegger was much less partisan with his judicial appointments than his predecessors (see Chapter 6).

In addition to the major formal authority discussed above, the governor has a wide range of other formal powers. He or she is commander in chief of the California National Guard, which on occasion is sent to help manage local crises in the state on a short-term basis. The governor also has the power to grant pardons, reprieves, or sentence commutations, although such authority is rarely exercised. Finally, the governor is the ceremonial head of state for greeting dignitaries from other countries. Along with the other major functions, these powers keep the governor on a fast track.

Informal Powers

Formal constraints on the governor can be offset to some extent by a power that is not written into the constitution at all: the governor's popularity. As the top state official, the governor is highly visible. The attention focused on the office provides a platform from which the governor can influence the public and overcome political opponents.

Historically, California's governors have used the prestige of their office to push their own agendas. Republican governor Pete Wilson touted **Proposition 187**, an attempt to reduce government benefits to illegal immigrants that was ultimately declared unconstitutional by the federal courts. In 1996 Wilson championed **Proposition 209**, titled the California Civil Rights Initiative, to eliminate affirmative action. And in 1998 he promoted **Proposition 227**, an initiative restricting bilingual education.

Democratic governor Gray Davis used his executive powers to relax the state's air standards during the 2001 state energy crisis, permitting older, dirtier electricity plants to produce more energy. When Davis was reelected in 2002, energy problems were compounded by a lengthy recession and huge budget shortfalls (see Chapter 8). But his inability to rely upon informal power stemmed from Davis's personality. He attacked the other branches of state government, claiming that state legislators were supposed to implement his vision[4] and that judicial appointees should reflect his views.[5] Further, his obsession with constant fund-raising from individuals and organizations in search of state business added

FIGURE 7.1 State Departments and Agencies.

to his image problems. In a July 2003 field poll, 61 percent of the respondents blamed Davis for the state's problems.[6] Thus, as an unprecedented recall effort moved along during 2003, Davis first lost his public support and informal power, and soon after that, his job.[7]

FIGURE 7.1 (Continued)

Arnold Schwarzenegger, in contrast, tried to use his informal powers both by schmoozing with and cajoling legislators and by appealing directly to the public. His record was mixed. He belittled the legislature, calling members "girlie men" for not adopting his budgets.[8] Sending the legislature into special session on sixteen occasions, rarely with any concrete plan, also did not win him friends among Democrats or Republicans. Frustrated, Schwarzenegger often went beyond the legislature to the chagrin of many members, cutting deals directly with organizations and institutions from local governments to universities, prison guards, and Indian gaming interests. Sometimes he prevailed, but other times he did not. Many of his item vetoes of "safety net" programs were overturned by the courts, yet his executive order to furlough state workers because of a budget shortfall was partially successful. And in 2010, Schwarzenegger worked out pension deals with several state employee unions that mandated higher employee contributions—something the legislature had not dared to even tackle.[9] In his own way, although clumsily at times, Schwarzenegger did attempt change.

Like Pete Wilson, Schwarzenegger went directly to the voters, but with mixed results. In March 2004 he barnstormed the state for Proposition 57, described as a $15 billion "recovery" bond, and **Proposition 58**, a measure designed to create more reserves in the future; both measures passed. But in 2005 Schwarzenegger suffered a major defeat, when he asked the voters to approve ballot measures on teacher tenure, union campaign contributions, strict state budget controls, and redistricting. So unpopular was the governor during this time that his standing in the public opinion polls plummeted from 64 percent to 35 percent in ten short months.[10] He never fully recovered.

Still, Schwarzenegger used his personality even in defeat to resurrect his standing with the public. Immediately after the election, he accepted full responsibility for the failed campaign, saying, "The buck stops with me." Using himself as the foil, the governor reflected, "I should have listened to my wife [prominent Democrat Maria Shriver], who said don't do this."[11] That kind of self-effacing approach allowed Schwarzenegger to begin anew with the voters and helped bring about reelection in 2006. But his ballot box success was short-lived. In 2009, Schwarzenegger placed his reputation on the line with support for a series of five budget-related legislative initiatives, all of which failed at the polls.

Ever-Changing Relationships

In the end, Schwarzenegger had an uneven relationship with the public. A blend of fiscal conservatism and social liberalism produced an antitax, antilabor governor who simultaneously was pro-choice, pro-health care, and pro-environment. His values may have lacked ideological consistency, but enough of them seemed to mesh with California's contradictory characteristics—especially his strong record on environmental protection. Still, Schwarzenegger's vision often exceeded his ability to deliver. In successive years, he declared the "year" of political reform, which ended with the defeat of four Schwarzenegger-tailored ballot measures; the "year" of health-care reform, which fizzled in the legislature; and the "year" of education reform, which sputtered out after he cut public funding several years in a row to leave California near the bottom of the fifty states in per capita spending.

Schwarzenegger's biggest political headache came from a poor relationship with members of his own political party. Particularly on social issues, he and the largely conservative Republican legislators had little agreement. Even on fiscal questions, Schwarzenegger and legislative Republicans had great difficulty forging a unified approach against the Democrats, as witnessed by his support for, and their resistance to, a state-funded health-care program, environmental protection legislation, and prison reform. Out of sync with his own party and never in sync with the Democrats, Arnold Schwarzenegger spent much of his governorship isolated from other leaders.

THE SUPPORTING CAST

If California's executive branch were composed solely of the governor, appointed department heads, and the civil service system, it would parallel the federal executive branch. However, the state's executive branch also includes a lieutenant governor, an attorney general, a secretary of state, a controller, a treasurer, an insurance commissioner, a superintendent of public instruction, and a five-member Board of Equalization. All are elected at the same time and serve four-year terms. Unlike the president and vice president, though, who are elected on the same political party ticket, each of these officeholders runs independently.

Most other states provide for the election of a lieutenant governor, a secretary of state, a treasurer, and an attorney general, but few elect an education officer, a controller, a Board of Equalization, and an insurance regulator. Moreover, most states call for the governor and the lieutenant governor (and others, in some cases) to run as a team, thus providing some executive branch cohesion. Not so in California, where each elected member of the executive branch is beholden to no one.

The consequences can be quite serious. For example, when Governor Schwarzenegger unilaterally withheld $3.1 billion for the public schools in 2005 in defiance of what many believed were state guarantees, Superintendent of Public Instruction Jack O'Connell sued. Ultimately, O'Connell dropped the suit after the governor and public school officials found agreement. In 2008 and 2010 Governor Schwarzenegger ordered reductions in the salaries of 200,000 state employees to the federal minimum wage ($6.55 per hour in 2008; $7.25 in 2010) until the legislature provided a budget. State Controller John Chiang, the individual responsible for issuing checks, refused to abide by the order, which he said exceeded Schwarzenegger's authority. Both times the courts found for the governor in principal, but an antiquated payroll system kept the controller from following through before the budget issue was resolved. On another occasion, then state insurance commissioner Steve Poizner sued to stop the sale of the state-run workers' compensation insurance fund, proposed by the governor to help balance the state budget. The issue languished in the courts long after Schwarzenegger and Poizner left office.[12] These examples show the extent to which very public fights can occur between two independently operating officeholders in the executive branch.

The Lieutenant Governor

The **lieutenant governor** is basically an executive-in-waiting with few formal responsibilities. If the governor becomes disabled or is out of the state, the lieutenant governor fills in as acting governor. If the governor leaves office, the lieutenant governor takes over. This has happened seven times in the state's history; the last time was in 1953, when Goodwin Knight replaced Earl Warren, who became chief justice of the United States Supreme Court. The current lieutenant governor, Democrat and former San Francisco Mayor Gavin Newsom, was elected in 2010, displacing Abel Maldonado, who had been appointed to the office earlier in the year.

The lieutenant governor heads some units, such as the State Lands Commission and the Commission on Economic Development, and is an ex officio member of the University of California Board of Regents and California State University Board of Trustees. He or she also serves as president of the state senate, but this job, too, is long on title and short on substance. As senate president, the lieutenant governor may vote to break ties, an event that last occurred in 1976. So minimal are the responsibilities of the lieutenant governor that an occupant of the office once quipped that his biggest daily task was to wake up, check the morning newspaper to see whether the governor had died, and then return to bed![13] That description may stretch the point a bit, but not by much. Still, the officeholder can be a nuisance to the governor, if nothing else. After a contentious budget battle in 2009 in which then Democratic lieutenant governor John Garamendi criticized Governor Schwarzenegger's management of the process, Schwarzenegger slashed Garamendi's office budget by 62 percent.

The Attorney General

Despite the lieutenant governor's higher rank, the **attorney general** is usually considered the second-most powerful member of the executive branch. As head of the Department of Justice, the attorney general oversees law enforcement activities, acts as legal counsel to state agencies, represents the state in important cases, and renders opinions on (interprets) proposed and existing laws. The current attorney general, Republican Steve Cooley, defeated San Francisco District Attorney Kamala Harris for the position in 2010. Previously, Cooley had served as district attorney in Los Angeles County longer than anyone in the county's history. He succeeds Jerry Brown, who served between 2006 and 2010.

Substantial authority and independent election allow the attorney general to chart a course separate from the governor's on important state questions. During his tenure as attorney general, for example, Jerry Brown sued insurance companies for misleading ads, prosecuted companies for not paying at least the minimum wage, and petitioned the federal government to regulate greenhouse gases. This same very public platform will allow Cooley to emphasize themes he mapped out earlier as district attorney. For example, Cooley long has advocated reform for California's "three strikes" law, which imposes long sentences on third-time lawbreakers, even if the third crime is a relatively harmless misdemeanor. No doubt, Cooley will be speaking out this and other issues.

The Secretary of State

Unlike the U.S. cabinet official who bears the same title, the **secretary of state** of California is basically a records keeper and elections supervisor. The job entails certifying the number and validity of signatures obtained for initiatives, referenda, and recall petitions; producing sample ballots and ballot arguments for the voters; publishing official election results; and keeping the records of the legislature and the executive branch. The current secretary of state, Democrat Debra Bowen, was first elected in 2006. She has brought order to an office that was rocked by scandal in 2005, when then secretary of state Kevin Shelley resigned because of a scandal involving illegal campaign contributions.

Recently, the secretary of state has had responsibility for converting California's election system from paper ballots to electronic voting machines. Bowen, a skeptic about electronic voting, has responsibility for modernizing the machines. She has been in no great hurry. In 2007 she announced a ban on almost all electronic voting machines in thirty-nine counties until it could be demonstrated that the machines are not prone to any viruses or manipulation.[14] This policy has required counties to either invest in new state-certified machines that include paper verification or resort to paper ballots.

The Superintendent of Public Instruction

The **superintendent of public instruction** heads the Department of Education. He or she is the only elected official in the executive branch chosen by nonpartisan ballot. Candidates are identified on the primary ballot only by their name and vocation. Unless one candidate wins a majority, the top two candidates face each other in the November general election. The current superintendent of public instruction, for State Senator and Assemblyman Tom Torlakson, was elected in 2010. While in the legislature, Torlakson was a champion of public education. During the fall 2010 campaign, he received strong support from the California Teachers' Association, the most powerful education organization in the state.

In general, the electorate knows little about the candidates for superintendent of public instruction, but teachers' unions, education administrators, and other affected groups take great interest in the choice of superintendent because this official oversees California's massive public education system. The superintendent's powers are severely limited, however—funding is determined largely by the governor's budgetary decisions, and policies are closely watched by the governor-appointed state board of education and the education committees of the legislature.

The Money Officers

Perhaps the most fractured part of the executive branch of California government is the group of elected officials who manage the state's money. Courtesy of the Progressive reformers who feared a concentration of power, the controller, the treasurer, and the Board of Equalization have separate but over-lapping responsibilities in this area. The **controller** supervises all state and local tax collection and writes checks for the state, including those to state employees. The controller is also an *ex officio* (automatic, by virtue of the office) member of several agencies, including the Board of Equalization, the Franchise Tax Board, and the State Lands Commission. Of all the "money officers," the controller is the most powerful, and thus the most prominent. The current controller, Democrat and former Board of Equalization member John Chiang, was elected in 2006 in his first run for statewide office and re-elected in 2010. From time to time, he has been outspoken on California's ongoing budget crisis.

The **treasurer** invests state funds raised through taxes and other means until they are needed for expenditures. The treasurer also borrows money for the state by issuing bonds approved by the voters. Typically amounting to several billion dollars, the bonds are sold in financial markets so that the state can finance long-term projects such as highways, water projects, or other infrastructure needs. The state then "redeems" the bonds over time through interest payments. Democrat Bill Lockyer, former state attorney general, was elected to this office in 2006 and re-elected in 2010. Unlike his predecessors, Lockyer has pushed the limits of his office by presenting periodic reports that reflect on the state's financial status with lending institutions that purchase California bonds.

The **Board of Equalization**, also part of California's fiscal system, oversees the collection of excise taxes on sales, gasoline, and liquor. The board also reviews county property assessment practices to ensure uniform calculation methods and practices. The board has five members—four of whom are elected in districts of equal population plus the controller.

Historically, the Board has attracted little attention. That changed in 2007, when the members voted to tax "alcopops"—sweet alcohol drinks often consumed by underage drinkers—at the same rate as hard liquor instead of beer. The change would have raised the tax from 20 cents per gallon to $3.30 per gallon and would have increased the cost of alcopop drinks by about 25 percent. But manufacturers avoided the tax by lowering the alcohol content below beer percentages. Still, the activism on the part of the Board of Equalization portended a new era for the tax agency.

The Insurance Commissioner

The office of **insurance commissioner** exemplifies the persistent reform mentality of California voters. Until 1988, the office was part of the state's Business, Housing, and Transportation Agency. However, with soaring insurance rates, voters approved an initiative that called for 20 percent across-the-board reductions in insurance premiums and created the elected position of insurance commissioner. ConsumerWatchdog, the public interest group behind the proposition, claims that the law saved California drivers more than $60 billion during its first twenty years of existence.

Democrat Dave Jones, a termed out member of the state assembly, was elected to the office in 2010, succeeding Steve Poizner, who elected to run for governor instead of seeking a second term. Known as a consumer advocate, Jones was named "2008 Consumer Champion" by the California Consumer Federation. He campaigned on the theme to hold health insurance companies accountable for any rate increases.

The Supporting Cast—Snow White's Seven Dwarfs?

Combined, the seven other elected members of the executive branch (plus the Board of Equalization) present an appearance of tremendous political activity. Still, their efforts often center on narrow policy areas and frequently are in opposition to one another, as well as to the much more powerful governor.

THE BUREAUCRACY

Elected officials are just the most observable part of the state's administrative machinery. Backing them up, implementing their programs, and dealing with citizens on a daily basis are about 335,000 state workers—the **bureaucracy**. Only about 5,000 of these workers are appointed by the governor or by other executive officers. Of the rest, 90,000 work at the University of California and California State University. The remainder are hired and fired through the state's **civil service system** on the basis of their examination results, performance, and job qualifications. The Progressives designed this system to insulate government workers from political influences and to make them more professional than those who might be hired out of friendship.

The task of the bureaucracy is to carry out the programs established by the policymaking institutions—the executive branch, the legislature, and the judiciary, along with a handful of regulatory agencies. However, because bureaucrats are permanent, full-time professionals, they sometimes influence the content of programs and policies, chiefly by advising public officials or by exercising the discretion built into the laws that define bureaucratic tasks. The bureaucracy can also influence policy through the lobbying efforts of its employee organizations (see Chapter 4).

State bureaucrats work for various departments and agencies (see Figure 7.1), each run by an administrator who is appointed by the governor and confirmed by the senate. Although civil servants are permanent employees, most administrators serve at the governor's pleasure and must resign at his or her demand. Sometimes, political appointees and civil servants clash over the best ways to carry out state policy. If the bureaucracy becomes too independent, the governor can always use his or her budgetary powers to bring it back into line or, in some cases, dismiss individual employees.

In recent years, California's bureaucrats have been particularly ambitious on climate change. The California Energy Commission has instituted energy efficiency standards for televisions and other electrical appliances. Also, the California Air Resources Board has led the way in regulating greenhouse gas levels.

These efforts have kept California's energy consumption flat during the past three decades, compared with a 40 percent increase in energy consumption nationwide.[15] They have also established California as a trendsetting state on the issues of global warming and energy use.

Some observers have criticized California's bureaucracy as unnecessarily inflated and unresponsive, even though the size of the state's system ranks forty-eighth of the fifty states on a per capita basis.[16] Still, there is no denying that slim or not, the state's bureaucracy has grown in recent years under the Schwarzenegger administration, despite his promise to "blow up the boxes" of the bureaucracy shortly after taking office. Between 2004 and 2008 the number of state employees per resident grew from 8.8 per thousand to 9.5 per thousand. Salary costs during the first five years of Schwarzenegger's governorship increased 37 percent, compared with 5 percent for a similar period under his predecessor, Gray Davis.[17] Clearly, there were differences between the governor's tough talk and reality.

MAKING THE PIECES FIT

The executive branch is a hodgepodge of independently elected authorities who serve in overlapping and conflicting institutional positions. Nobody, not even the governor, is really in charge. Each official simply attempts to carry out his or her mission with the hope that passable policy will result. Occasionally, reformers have suggested streamlining the system by consolidating functions and reducing the number of elective offices, but the only recent change has been the addition of yet another office, that of insurance commissioner.

Despite these obstacles, the officeholders—most notably governors—have been active policymakers. Pete Wilson waged war against illegal immigrants, affirmative action, and welfare while trumpeting the "law and order" theme. Gray Davis responded to the state's power shortage crisis. Arnold Schwarzenegger was instrumental in environmental reform.

Still, the governor does not operate in a vacuum. He or she must contend with other members of the executive branch, a fractured and suspicious legislature, independent courts, a professional bureaucracy, and most of all, an electorate with a highly erratic collective pulse. Whether these conditions are challenges or impediments, they make the executive branch a fascinating element of California government.

NOTES

1. "Gov. Calls for New Spending on Prisons," *Los Angeles Times*, June 27, 2006, pp. A1, A7.

2. "Special Sessions Define Schwarzenegger," Sign on San Diego, October 22, 2009, http://signonsandiego.printthis.clickability.com/pt/cpt?action=cpt&tit.

3. "Judge Halts Many State Furloughs," *San Francisco Chronicle*, March 25, 2010, pp. A1, A12.

4. "Tensions Flare between Davis and His Democrats," *Los Angeles Times*, July 22, 1999, pp. A1, A28.

5. "Davis Comments Draw Fire," *San Jose Mercury News*, March 1, 2000, p. 14A.

6. *The Field Poll*, Release #2074, July 15, 2003.

7. For an account of how Davis fell from power, see Larry N. Gerston and Terry Christensen, *Recall! California's Political Earthquake* (Armonk, N.Y.: M. E. Sharpe, 2004).

8. "Gov. Criticizes Legislators as 'Girlie Men,'" *Los Angeles Times*, July 18, 2004, pp. B1, B18.

9. "Governor Slashes Workers' Pay," *San Francisco Chronicle,* July 2, 2010, pp. C1, C6.

10. "Schwarzenegger's Popularity Slide," *Los Angeles Times*, October 28, 2005, p. B2.

11. "Schwarzenegger Says the Fault Is His," *New York Times*, November 11, 2006, p. A14.

12. "Plan to Sell Portion of State Fund Collapses," *Los Angeles Times*, December 30, 2009, pp. B1, B5.

13. "The Most Invisible Job in Sacramento," *Los Angeles Times*, May 10, 1998, pp. A1, A20.

14. "Touch Vote Machine Ban Hurts Counties, *San Francisco Chronicle*, August 7, 2007, p. B3.

15. "California Imposes Rule for Efficiency on Some TVs," *New York Times*, November 19, 2009, p. A16.

16. "Looking for Waste," *Economist*, May 1, 2010, p. 33.

17. "Soaring Payroll Stymies 'Reform' Governor," *San Francisco Chronicle*, May 28, 2008, pp. A1, A6.

LEARN MORE ON THE WEB

Office of the Attorney General:
www.caag.state.ca.us

Office of the Governor:
www.gov.ca.gov

Office of the Secretary of State:
www.ss.ca.gov

Office of the State Board of Equalization:
www.boe.ca.gov

Office of the State Controller:
www.sco.ca.gov

Office of the State Insurance Commissioner:
www.insurance.ca.gov

Office of the State Treasurer:
www.treasurer.ca.gov

Office of the State Superintendent of Public Instruction:
www.cde.ca.gov/eo

Salaries of state employees:
www.capitolweekly.net/salaries/index.php?_c=yzbexjathf9ge0

LEARN MORE AT THE LIBRARY

John C. Bollens and G. Robert Williams. *Jerry Brown in a Plain Brown Wrapper.* Pacific Palisades, Calif.: Palisades Publishers, 1978.

Larry N. Gerston and Terry Christensen. *Recall! California's Political Earthquake.* Armonk, N.Y.: M. E. Sharpe, 2004.

Gary G. Hamilton and Nicole Woolsey Biggert. *Governor Reagan, Governor Brown: A Sociology of Executive Power.* New York: Columbia University Press, 1984.

Joe Mathews. *The People's Machine.* New York: Public Affairs Press, 2006.

8

Taxing and Spending: Budgetary Politics and Policies

CHAPTER CONTENTS

No issue is more critical to Californians than taxation, and no resource is more important to state policymakers than the revenues generated from taxation. Those dollars become the foundation of the annual state budget, the document that determines where and how state funds will be spent.

The connection between taxing and spending can be difficult. Even though most people may agree on taxes in principle, they often disagree on how much should be collected and from whom, as well as who the recipients of those funds should be. When policymakers seem to stray from general public values on budgetary issues, the voters are not shy about using direct democracy to reorder the state's fiscal priorities—and with so many more policy areas of need than dollars available, much is at stake.

CALIFORNIA'S BUDGET ENVIRONMENT

Unlike the national government, which usually operates with a deficit, states are required to balance their budgets. This has been difficult in California, where a steady flow of immigrants, a burgeoning school-aged population, massive attention to crime, and deteriorating infrastructure make for a challenging budget environment. Since a recession in 2002, the state has struggled with one projected state revenue deficit after another regardless of who has been in power. An astronomical projected deficit in 2003 no doubt contributed to the recall of then governor Gray Davis. The state languished in fiscal crisis.

All of that was supposed to change with the fresh approach of Arnold Schwarzenegger. Relying on federal assistance, deferred expenditures, and income sources not even considered by the legislature, Schwarzenegger promised a "balanced" budget. In fact, his first budget was $8 billion out of balance immediately upon signature, according to the state legislative analyst.[1] A temporary economic upswing in 2006 helped the governor and state legislature reach agreement on a balanced, on-time budget for the first time in years. But the joy was short-lived.

By 2008, the state faced a revenue shortfall in excess of $15 billion, once again forcing state leaders to consider drastic cuts, major tax increases, or a combination of the two. In the end, legislators and the governor agreed to a gimmicky document that was "balanced" in name only. In fact, the budget was the most unbalanced in state history. Twice in 2009, the governor and legislature grappled with the deficit. First, they sutured a massive $42 billion hole in March through a combination of new taxes, program cuts, and transfers. Three months later, state leaders had to overcome a new $24 billion gap—this time in program and services cuts only. These events occurred because of a terribly weak state economy, which led to reduced tax revenues and increased demands for social services. Much of the "fix" centered on deferred maintenance, withholding of local government redevelopment funds, and higher withholding of state income taxes. Budget makers even delayed payment of state employee paychecks from June 30 to July 1 so they could "save" $900 million.[2]

The state's economic malaise continued into the 2010–2011 fiscal year, when the weary governor and legislature faced a new $21 billion hole. Again they cut. As a result, California's state budget has shrunk from about $105 billion in 2005–2006 to $83 billion in 2010–2011, even though the state's population has grown from 36 million to 38.6 million.

The voters haven't helped with this ongoing dilemma. Repeatedly, the public has rejected new taxes while embracing new programs and services—the kind of logic that has California in its present-day bind. When two Field polls in March 2010 asked the best way to balance the state budget, respondents who favored spending cuts outnumbered those who favored tax increases by a margin of nearly 4 to 1.[3] Yet when survey respondents were asked where the cuts should be made, majorities could be found in only two of fourteen major public policy areas—prisons and parks.[4] Moreover, over the past quarter century, voters have passed a series of ballot propositions directing the state to spend money on various programs ranging from longer prison sentences to more comprehensive public education without providing the funds. This is the political environment in which elected officials must make tough decisions.

THE BUDGETARY PROCESS

Budget making is a complicated and lengthy activity in California. Participants include the governor and various executive-branch departments, the legislature and its support agencies, the public (via initiative and referendum), and increasingly, the courts when judges uphold or overturn commitments made by the other policymakers.

The Governor and Other Executive Officers

Preparation of the annual budget is the governor's most important formal power. Other policymakers participate in the budgetary process, but no other individual has as much clout. The governor frames the document before it goes to the legislature and then has additional say afterward through use of the item veto on budget items that he or she opposes. Given this unique power position, legislative leaders often negotiate with the chief executive over what he or she will accept long before the budget lands on the governor's desk.

During the summer and fall, the governor's director of finance works closely with the budget heads of each state agency. Supported by a staff of fiscal experts and researchers, the director of finance gathers and assesses information about the anticipated needs of each department and submits a "first draft" budget to the governor in late fall. The governor presents a refined version of this draft to the legislature the following January. The state constitution gives the legislature until June 15 to respond. The annual budget is supposed to take effect on July 1, but as we learned in Chapter 5, on-time delivery is anything but routine.

Legislative Participants

Upon receiving the budget in January, the legislature's leaders do little more than refer the document to the legislative analyst. Over the next two months, the legislative analyst and his or her staff scrutinize each part of the budget, considering needs, costs, and other factors. Often, the analyst's findings clash with those of the governor, providing the legislature with an independent source of data and evaluation.

Meanwhile, two key legislative units in each house—the appropriations committees and the budget committees—guide the budget proposal through the legislative process. After the staffs of these committees spend about two months going through the entire document, each house assigns portions to various other committees and their staffs. During this time, lobbyists, individual citizens, government officials, and other legislators testify on the proposed budget before committees and subcommittees. By mid-April, the committees conclude their hearings, combine their portions into a single document, and bring the budget bill to their respective full house for a vote.

As June nears and the two houses hone their versions, a select group of leaders enter into informal negotiations over the document. Known as the **Big Five**, the governor, the speaker of the assembly, the president pro tem of the senate, and the minority party leaders of each house become the nucleus of the final budgetary decisions. In recent years, the Big Five have cast long shadows over just about all of the other players. Should the two houses differ on specifics, the bill goes to a two-house conference committee for reconciliation, after which both houses vote again. Because of a voter-passed initiative in 2010, it now takes a simple majority to pass the budget, a change from the previous long-standing two-thirds requirement. However, inasmuch as a two-thirds vote is still required for revenue increases, the significance of this change is questionable.

The Courts

Sometimes, the courts weigh in on key budget issues to address some of the "quick fixes" to complex budget issues enacted by public policymakers or the voters. Governor Schwarzenegger was humbled in 2005 when a state superior court judge ruled that he was obligated to enforce a new law that reduced the ratio of patients to nurses from 6–1 to 5–1. In 2008, a decision by the U.S. District Court forced the state to spend billions of dollars on improved prison conditions, adding still more to a budget already billions in the red. In 2009 a federal court rejected $500 million in social service cuts as incompatible with federal law, a decision that added to the budget crisis of that year. And even as California attempted to comply with a federal court order to reduce the inmate population of its overcrowded state prisons, a court-appointed receiver rejected the state's effort to reduce costs as excessive. Clearly, the courts have found reason to shape state budgets.[5]

Even the will of the voters has been subject to judicial review on matters relating to the state budget. Particularly significant have been the many cases arising from Proposition 13. Also, decisions on the famous "three strikes and you're out" initiative (see Chapter 6) have added greatly to state incarceration costs.

The Public

On occasion, the public shapes the budget through initiatives or referenda. The voters relied on ballot propositions to approve the sales tax (1933) and repeal the inheritance tax (1982).

In 1993 the voters passed a proposition that increased the state sales tax by 0.5 percent, with new revenues exclusively earmarked for public safety provided by local governments. In 2004 the voters enacted an initiative that created an additional 1 percent tax bracket for people with taxable incomes of $1 million or more, with the funds designated for mental health programs. The public doesn't always agree to increases, however. The voters soundly rejected a 2006 initiative that would have added an additional tax bracket of 1.7 percent beyond the highest level for individuals with taxable incomes of $400,000 or more, with the revenues earmarked for a statewide preschool program.

In 2009, the governor and legislature strung together five ballot proposals that would simultaneously cap spending and temporarily increase sales taxes (0.25 percent), income taxes (1 percent) and motor vehicle fees (0.50 percent). The ballot proposals also would have earmarked half of any extra revenues to the public schools. The package also would have given the governor new powers to cut programs midyear. The public said no to all five propositions.

Perhaps the most dramatic tax-altering event came in 1978 with the passage of **Proposition 13**, an initiative that reduced local property taxes by 57 percent. Since then, property owners have saved more than $528 billion in taxes,[6] while local governments have become increasingly dependent on the state for relief. As a result, the state has become the major funder for local services such as public education, although support has varied with the health of the economy. This uncertainty has brought endless criticism from local government officials.

The bottom line is that there are many more players in the budget process than meet the eye. This complexity both slows down the process and requires near unanimity among the various parties before any major decisions are made.

REVENUE SOURCES

Like most states, California relies on several forms of taxation to fund its general fund budget (that is, the budget exclusive of federal funds). The largest sources of revenue are personal income tax, sales tax, and bank and corporation taxes. Smaller revenue supplies come from motor vehicle, fuel, insurance, tobacco, and alcohol taxes. The state's major revenue sources and expenditures for fiscal year 2010–2011 are shown in Figure 8.1.

Other taxes are levied by local governments. Chief among these is the property tax, although its use was reduced considerably by Proposition 13. This tax is collected by counties rather than by the state, but the state allocates it among the different levels of local government, and it still is a part—directly or indirectly— of the tax burden of all Californians.

All too aware of the state's antitax mood, policymakers have refused to add taxes to cope with burgeoning needs. As a result, the state's commitments to most services have decreased considerably over the past three decades. Individual recipients, school districts, and local governments have been thrown into

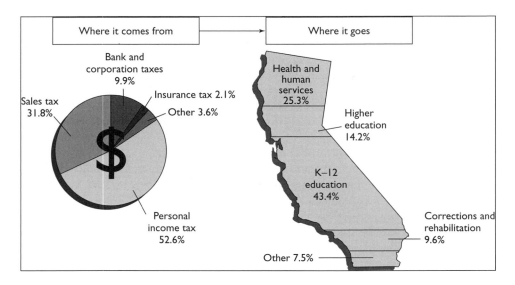

FIGURE 8.1 California's Revenue Sources and Expenditures, 2010–2011

turmoil. Infrastructure work, such as repairs after the 1989 and 1994 earthquakes, and certain highway maintenance programs have been stretched out. Placement of a new earthquake-resistant Oakland–San Francisco Bay bridge will not be complete until 2013, twenty-four years after the earthquake that caused its damage. In fact, a recent study ranks California forty-seventh of the fifty states in per capita highway expenditures.[7]

The Sales Tax

Until the Great Depression of 1929, a relatively small state government garnered funds by relying on minor taxes on businesses and utilities. After the economic crash, however, the state was forced to develop new tax sources to cope with hard times. The first of these, a 2.5 percent **sales tax**, was adopted to provide permanent funding for schools and local governments. Today, the statewide sales tax is 8.25 percent. Of that amount, cities and counties get 2 percent to help meet health and public safety needs. The state keeps the rest. In addition, as much as 1.5 percent is tacked on by counties engaged in state-approved projects, most of which are transportation related.

Occasionally, changes take place in response to economic conditions. In 1991, Governor Pete Wilson and the legislature cut the sales tax by 0.25 percent when the state enjoyed a huge budget surplus. This reduction remained in place until 2002, when the revenue shortfall forced an adjustment upward. In response to the budget crisis in 2004, Governor Schwarzenegger persuaded voters to approve Proposition 57, which provided $15 billion in bonds, or borrowed money, to be repaid over the next decade by diverting 0.25 percent of local governments' share of the sales tax. Today, the sales tax accounts for about 31.8 percent of the state's tax revenues.

The Personal Income Tax

A second major revenue source, the **personal income tax**, was modeled after its federal counterpart to collect greater amounts of money from those residents with greater earnings. Today, the personal income tax varies between 1.0 and 10.3 percent, depending on one's income. The last revision was in 2004, when voters approved a ballot proposition that added a 1 percent tax to those Californians with incomes of $1 million or more. That money is earmarked for mental health programs.

The personal income tax is now the fastest-growing component of state revenue (see Figure 8.2)—a significant fact because Californians ranked tenth among the fifty states in per capita income in 2009. Inasmuch as the tax goes up with increasing incomes, it filled the state coffers in the dramatic economic boom during the later part of the 1990s and slowed just as dramatically in the first few years of the twenty-first century. As of 2010, the personal income tax accounted for 52.6 percent of the state tax bite.

Bank and Corporation Taxes

Financial industry and corporation income taxes contribute much less to California's budget than do sales and personal income taxes. Taxes on bank and

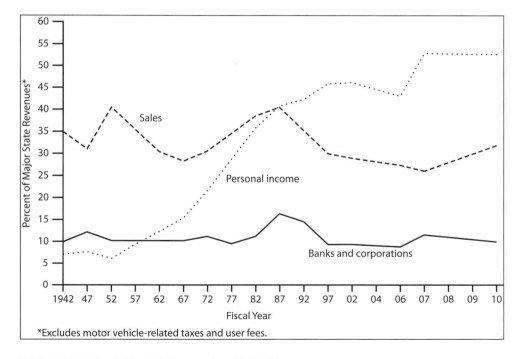

FIGURE 8.2   California's Tax Burden, 1948–2011

corporate incomes did not exceed 5.5 percent until 1959, when the legislature enacted the first of a series of rate hikes. The last increase occurred in 1980, when, responding to local governments' losses from Proposition 13, the legislature boosted the **bank and corporation tax** from 9.6 percent to 11.6 percent. Between 1987 and 1996, however, the legislature reduced the tax to 8.84 percent, where it remains for corporations today. Since 1996 the corporate tax for banks has been fixed at 10.84 percent. Together, bank and corporation taxes now account for about 9.9 percent of state revenues.

Aside from Proposition 13 and the expanded reliance on **user taxes**, such as those levied on gasoline and cigarettes, California's revenue collection system has undergone gradual adjustments over the past sixty years. Figure 8.2 shows the changing weight of the sales, personal income, and bank and corporation taxes from 1942 to the present. Recent data indicate a steady drift toward increased dependence on the personal income tax and decreased dependence on sales and corporation taxes, although the recession of 2008–2010 pushed income tax receipts down somewhat, while sales taxes increased.

Other Sources

From time to time, state leaders have asked voters to approve bonds, thus obligating the electorate to long-term commitments. These projects, sometimes lasting as long as forty years, finance major infrastructure commitments such as school classroom, transportation, and water projects.

The state has turned to bonds with increasing frequency. In 1991, California ranked thirty-second among the fifty states in indebtedness on a per capita basis. By 2009, the state's bond debt increased to more than $140 billion, $70 billion of which had been enacted during the Schwarzenegger administration alone. That represents a per capita indebtedness of $1,805—well above the national average.

California also gets a small but growing portion of its revenue from fees and charges for services. For example, 90 percent of the operating costs of state parks were funded by taxes in 1982–1983, but within a decade, only 40 percent came from tax revenues, while 57 percent came from fees and concessions. Although Governor Davis and the legislature reduced those fees in 2000, new budget pressures led Governor Schwarzenegger and the legislature to increase them again in 2004 and 2008.

Taxes in Perspective

Viewed in a comparative context, the overall tax burden for California ranks ninth in the nation on a per capita basis, remarkably close to its per capita income ranking. Nevertheless, there have been changes in the state tax blend, with the state becoming increasingly dependent on the personal income tax as its primary source of income.

When calculating state and local taxes as a percentage of personal income, California ranks thirteenth. On a per capita basis, the state ranks seventeenth in sales taxes, eighth in personal income taxes, seventh in bank and corporation taxes, and twenty-ninth in property taxes.[8]

In other areas, California taxes are near the bottom, due largely to the influence of powerful interest groups. For example, the state ranks forty-ninth in both fuel taxes and alcoholic beverage taxes. Reformers attempted to establish oil production taxes of $400 million over ten years via initiative in 2006, but the measure was soundly defeated at the polls. As a result, California is the only one of fourteen major oil-producing states that does not tax oil. With respect to tobacco taxes, California ranks thirty-third in the nation.[9] Had the voters approved a ballot proposition in 2006 increasing the tobacco tax by $2.60 per pack, the state would be collecting an additional $2 billion for children's health care—but that measure, too, was defeated. In these and other cases, interest groups have carried great sway with the legislature and public.

SPENDING

The annual state budget addresses thousands of financial commitments, both large and small. Major areas of expenditure include public education (grades K through 12), health and welfare, higher education, and prisons. Outlays in these four areas account for nearly 90 percent of the general fund. The remainder of the budget (the difference between total expenditures and the general fund) goes to designated long-term projects such as transportation, parks, and veterans' programs, many of which have been authorized by public ballot.

Since 1979 state spending has been determined more by the public than by the legislature and the governor. Under Proposition 4 (1979) and Proposition 111 (1990), budgets have been determined largely by formulas rather than by need. In 2004—again at the urging of Governor Schwarzenegger—the voters passed **Proposition 58**, which requires the state to gradually set aside up to 3 percent of all revenues in a "rainy day" fund, beginning in 2006. Some critics have characterized the formula approach as a political "straitjacket" that is unresponsive to changing times and needs; others have viewed it as inconsequential, since the state rarely has enjoyed any surplus. Defenders of "formula government" argue that it is the only way to keep state leaders from operating with a blank check.

Push came to shove in 2008. As Democrats and Republicans battled over whether to increase taxes or cut expenditures, the governor waited in frustration for a budget that eventually reached his desk a record eighty days late. Yet all that paled in comparison to the budget crisis in 2009. Confronted with a $42 billion deficit, the governor and legislature asked the voters to help bridge the gap by passing a series of temporary tax increases and tougher spending rules. The voters declined for a variety of reasons. Some argued that they were overtaxed already; others didn't like the extent to which the governor would have had increased budget-making authority with little legislative oversight; others still rejected more creative borrowing, this time through future revenues from the state lottery.[10] The result was that the legislature and governor made massive spending cuts.

More cuts, though less dramatic, were made in 2010 after the budget came in one hundred days late—yet another dubious record. Some observers noted that the damage to education and social welfare programs was not as bad as in the past, but others were quick to point out that the reductions only compounded the cuts that have occurred over the past several years.

Public Education: Grades K through 12

The state constitution gives public education a "superior right" to state funds; as such, public schools get the largest share of the state budget. Local school districts periodically add relatively small amounts to education through voter-approved bonds and parcel taxes, but the preponderance of support comes from the state legislature through its annual allocations.

Funding for public education in California has an uneven history. The state ranked among the top-funded states throughout the 1950s and 1960s. Then the pattern changed. During the 1970s and 1980s, the state consistently reduced its per capita support for K through 12 public education, shrinking it to 37 percent of the general fund in 1988. That same year, amid growing concerns about weak funding and poor classroom performance, education reformers secured voter approval of **Proposition 98**, a measure that established 40 percent as a minimum funding threshold except in times of fiscal emergency. With this mandate, the state poured money into reducing class sizes in grades K through 3 and lengthened the school year from 180 to 190 days. But the upward direction was short lived.

State aid for public education has dropped precipitously with declining state revenues. Between 2008 and 2010 alone, support fell from $50.3 billion to $44.6 billion, a drop of $470 per student; per capita spending dropped more than another $400 after completion of the 2010-2011 budget. At $8,784 per student (2008–2009 figures), California expenditures remain about $1,900 below the national average. According to former state superintendent of public instruction Jack O'Connell, California now ranks forty-sixth of the fifty states in per capita expenditures—despite having one of the highest per capita incomes in the nation (see Figure 8.3).[11] Meanwhile, the school year minimum has fallen to 175 days—three full weeks less classroom instruction than fifteen years ago.

California continues to be near the bottom (forty-ninth) among the states in its student-teacher ratio (a commonly used criterion for assessing education effectiveness) and in reading achievement. The state also ranks forty-seventh in the number of computers per classroom. All this has produced a sorry, if not unexpected, outcome in terms of high school graduation. As of 2010 the state ranked forty-eighth in high school graduation rates.[12] According to studies by the National Assessment of Educational Progress, a well-known nonprofit group, California hovers near the bottom of almost every assessment category. Table 8.1 shows the most recent data available.

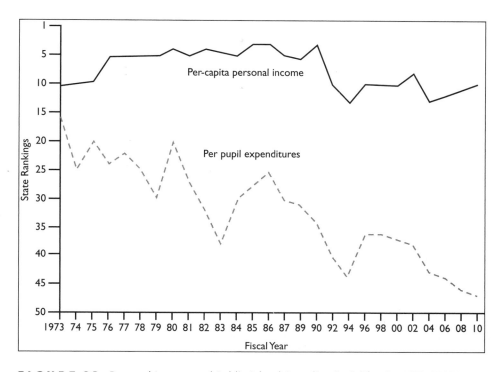

FIGURE 8.3 Personal Income and Public School Spending in California, 1973–2008

TABLE 8.1 California Rankings in Key Education Categories

Category	Rank	Year
Reading, 4th grade	49th	2009
Math, 4th grade	44th	2009
Math, 8th grade	48th	2009
Science, 8th grade	42d	2005*

*Only 44 states participated in the 8th grade science survey.
SOURCE: National Assessment of Education Progress, 2010.

With Latino and Asian American students accounting for 49 percent and 12 percent of the school population, respectively, language-related issues have emerged. In 1998 the passage of **Proposition 227**, a measure limiting bilingual education for non-English–speaking students to one year, added to the debate over how to "mainstream" the diverse California student community. All of this has occurred in a state where one-fourth of all public school students are "English learners" (English is not the first language), compared with 9 percent nationally.

There are chilling consequences from these policies. For starters, California has a high-school dropout rate of 24 percent, or about 125,000 students annually.[13] With few skills, their futures are very limited. At the other end of the spectrum, large numbers of those who do graduate high school are unprepared for college. A recent California State University study found that 55 percent of the incoming freshman class needed remedial instruction in either English or math.[14] Neither of these statistics points to educational excellence.

Nevertheless, the debate goes on. Some reformers have turned to "charter schools"—independent, community-controlled alternatives to what many describe as a broken system. As of 2010 there were about 800 charter schools in California—still a small number compared with the state's 9,700 traditional public schools, although up from 600 in 2008. Other reformers have promoted vouchers—cash payments for parents to use in selecting an educational institution—but the voters have rejected such measures twice in recent years.

The process of fixing California's public education problems will be neither quick nor cheap. In 2007 a 1,700-page report commissioned by Governor Arnold Schwarzenegger declared that it would cost a staggering $1.5 trillion more each year to make all students academically proficient in traditional core knowledge areas such as reading, math, and science.[15] With current state and local expenditures for public education in the neighborhood of $75 billion, even the first step in such a leap would seem highly unlikely.

Higher Education: Colleges and Universities

California's budget woes have cut deeply into support for higher education. Once viewed as the role model for public universities,[16] the higher education system has suffered for a lack of funding and greatly reduced admission slots.

Three components share responsibility for higher education in the state. The state's 110 two-year community colleges enroll about 2.9 million students. Historically, community colleges have been viewed as the entry institutions for students who otherwise did not qualify for, or who could not afford to attend, California's four-year public universities. Funding for these community colleges is connected to the formula for primary and secondary public schools; to that extent, they have benefited from Proposition 98. Still, reduced budget allocations from the state have forced the community colleges to pare back instruction offerings. As a result, during the 2009–2010 academic year, community colleges turned away approximately 140,000 students.[17]

With 222,000 students, the University of California (UC) educates both undergraduate and graduate students at ten campuses throughout the state. Designated as the state's primary research university, UC is the only public institution permitted to award professional degrees (such as medical and law degrees) and doctorates. The California State University (CSU) system, with 433,000 students at twenty-three campuses, concentrates on undergraduate instruction, awarding master's degrees most commonly in such fields as education, engineering, and business.

State support for public universities was fairly constant until the 1990s, holding at about 11 percent of the general-fund budget, and it peaked at 12.7 percent during the 2002–2003 fiscal year. Support eroded considerably during the budget crisis that followed, with the state allocation resting at about 11.7 percent of the general fund in 2008–2009. More significantly, the state's share of the cost of education has decreased dramatically. For example, whereas California provided 90 percent of UC's education costs in 1969–1970, support dropped to 62 percent in 2009–2010. And at CSU, the 90 percent paid by the state in 1969–1970 fell to 69 percent in 2009–2010. Students have been forced to make up much of the shortfall. At both UC and CSU, student fees have more than doubled between 2003–2004 and 2010–2011. Meanwhile, CSU has cut back new enrollments by 40,000; UC has reduced enrollments by 1,500. Between tuition increases and the lack of room, the college participation rate of nineteen-year-olds has fallen precipitously—from 43 percent to 30 percent between 1996 and 2004 alone, dropping California from 17th to 46th place among the 50 states.[18]

Health and Human Services

Health and human services programs receive the second-largest share of the state budget. The programs accounting for the most significant state commitment include California Work Opportunity and Responsibility to Kids (CalWORKS), Medi-Cal, and the Supplemental Security Income (SSI) program. Medi-Cal provides health-care benefits for the poor, and SSI offers state assistance to the elderly and the disabled. But no program is as politically charged as CalWORKS, the primary welfare program.

California has sizable welfare costs. With about 12 percent of the nation's population, the state is home to 25 percent of all welfare recipients. In 1990, in contrast, California had 10.5 percent of the nation's population and 12 percent of all welfare recipients.

As welfare numbers have increased, per capita spending has gone down. Changes in state policy began in 1997 after Congress passed the Welfare Reform Act, limiting welfare payments to no more than five years. Shortly thereafter, the legislature passed its CalWORKS legislation, which provides cash grants and welfare-to-work services for needy families with children ten years of age or younger and requires all adults to work at least thirty-two hours per week. As of 2010, about 1.3 million Californians were CalWORKS recipients, two-thirds of whom were children. For the 2010–2011 budget, Governor Schwarzenegger proposed an end to CalWORKS. Elimination would have saved the state budget $1.6 billion annually, although California would have lost $4 billion in matching federal funds. The legislature rejected Schwarzenegger's proposal, although benefits were trimmed. Every other state has a welfare-to-work program.

As of 2010, health and human services programs accounted for about 25 percent of the general fund. Average monthly welfare payments were less than $500 for the typical family of three, down by one-third from five years earlier. Still, with the state scrambling to close a $21 billion budget hole for the coming fiscal year, Governor Schwarzenegger proposed cutting in-home health care for the elderly and disabled by one-third to save $6.04 billion. As with CalWORKS, the legislature greatly tempered the governor's proposal.

Prisons

Of the major state allocation categories, the budgets for prisons and corrections have grown the most in recent years. As with education, the public has played a role in this policy area. Several initiatives have established mandatory prison terms for various crimes and extended the terms for many other crimes. Even more sweeping changes occurred in 1994, when the legislature (and later the voters, through an initiative) enacted a new **"three strikes"** law. This new law required a sentence of twenty-five years to life for anyone convicted of three felonies and added more than 43,000 long-term prisoners to the corrections system between 1994 and 2004.

As a result of the three-strikes law and other policy changes, California's prison population has swelled beyond belief. In 1994 the total prison population was 125,000; it had jumped to 168,000 by 2009—more than double the official capacity. Currently, the costs for incarceration average $49,000 per convict per year. The demographics are equally interesting: 37 percent Latino, 27 percent African American, and 27 percent white. Phenomenal incarceration growth has forced the construction of new prisons, such as the new prison in Delano in 2005. Still, with a soaring inmate population, in 2006 Governor Schwarzenegger asked the legislature to build at least two more state prisons at a cost of $500 million each.[19]

About 10 percent of the state's general fund was used for corrections and rehabilitation during the 2009–2010 fiscal year—once again reflecting the sharpest increase of any major budget category. Meanwhile, lawsuits have led federal court orders requiring the state to release as many as 40,000 prisoners by 2012. Should that occur, the prison budget may moderate.

Other Budget Obligations

California's budget crisis has many sources, some obvious and others not. Clearly, a prolonged recession has contributed mightily to the state's revenue grief. On the expenditure side of the budget ledger, out-of-control prison spending has been of great concern. Two other less known, yet fast-growing state expenditure categories are payment of bond debt and pension payouts. Together, they now consume more than 10 percent of the state general fund and show little sign of slowing down.

Bonds   While voter-approved borrowing through bonds represents an "easy" way to fund major projects over time, cumulatively these bonds are taking a toll on the state. California now ranks tenth in per capita bond debt, up from thirty-second in 1991. Our propensity to rely upon bonds has generated the lowest credit rating of any state, which adds to the interest costs to retire the bonds. About 6.7 percent of the state budget now goes to paying interest on the debt. Moreover, State Treasurer Bill Lockyer estimated in 2009 that at present rates, 10 percent or more of the state budget will be dedicated to debt payment by the middle of this decade.[20] The state's propensity for financing through bonds has left it with the lowest bond rating of any state, which means the highest interest payments.[21]

Retirement Pensions   California's massive public employee pension program, the California Public Employees' Retirement System (CalPERS), covers more than 1.6 million employees, retirees, and their families, or about 4 percent of the state's population. Just under 500,000 are retirees who have worked for various state government agencies. Employees contribute a small portion of their salary to the program, with the state providing the rest as part of the salary compensation package. For years CalPERS gushed with surpluses, thanks to a robust financial market that contained most of the fund's investments. Since the onslaught of the recession in 2008, CalPERS payments have exceeded revenues. By law, the state must make up for any shortfall, and that money comes out of the state budget. In fiscal year 2009–2010, the state was required pay out 5.6 percent of the general fund into CalPERS—up dramatically from a figure that historically averaged 3.4 percent.

CALIFORNIA'S BUDGET: TOO LITTLE, TOO MUCH, OR JUST RIGHT?

Have you ever met anyone who claims that he or she should pay more taxes? Neither have we. Almost everybody dislikes paying taxes, and almost everybody thinks that the money collected is spent incorrectly or unwisely. That seems to be a perennial dilemma in California. However, although most people oppose increased taxes, they also oppose program cuts. It's a modern-day dilemma for state policymakers and the public alike.

   Like their counterparts elsewhere, California policymakers have struggled to find a fair system of taxation to pay for needed programs. Given the involvement of so many public and private interests, however, it's difficult to determine what is fair. Moreover, during the last few decades, taxation and budget decisions have been subject to radical change. Somehow, the state's infrastructure has survived, although critics have been less than thrilled with the fiscal uncertainty that has become commonplace in California government.

NOTES

1. "Debt Remains in Governor's Budget Plan," *San Jose Mercury News*, July 1, 2004, pp. 1A, 17A.
2. "Deal Puts State in Hole for Next Year," *San Francisco Chronicle*, July 26, 2009, pp. A1, A17.

3. Field Poll, Release No. 2329, March 2, 2010.

4. Field Poll, Release No. 2335, March 24, 2010.

5. "California Finding That Prisons Costs Aren't So Easy to Cut," *San Jose Mercury News*, March 24, 2010, pp. B1, B9.

6. Howard Jarvis Taxpayers Association, 2009, www.hjta.org/index.php.

7. "Highway Spending," in *Governing: State and Local Sourcebook* (Washington, D.C.: Congressional Quarterly, 2006), pp. 32–36.

8. "Finance," in *Governing: State and Local Government Sourcebook* (Washington, D.C.: Congressional Quarterly, 2006), pp. 32–36.

9. "State Cigarette Excise Tax Rates and Rankings, 2010," www.tobaccofreekids.org.

10. See "Ballot Battle to Follow Wrangling over Budget," *San Francisco Chronicle*, February 17, 2009, pp. A1, A14; and "Traditional Foes Team Up over Prop. 1A," *San Francisco Chronicle*, April 6, 2009, pp. A1, A7.

11. Testimony before Assembly Budget Subcommittee No. 2, March 11, 2008.

12. See *Just the Facts* (Albany: Public Policy Institute of New York State, 2007).

13. "State Education Rankings: Graduation Rates for High School, College and Grad/ Professional School," Associated Content, July 21, 2010, www.associatedcontent .com/article/5562698/state_education_rankings_graduation.html

14. "CSU Freshmen Face Challenges," *Los Angeles Times*, March 15, 2006, p. B9.

15. "No Quick, Cheap Fix for State's Schools," *Los Angeles Times*, March 15, 2007, pp. B1, B10.

16. See James Richardson, "What Price Glory?" *UCLA Magazine*, February 1997, p. 30; also see "A Crown Jewel of Education Struggles with Cuts in California," *New York Times*, November 20, 2009, pp. A1, A25.

17. "Community Colleges Make Concerted Effort to Meet Demand," press release issued by the California Community Colleges Chancellor's Office, Sacramento, June 3, 2010.

18. Christopher Neufeld and Stanton Glantz, "Ending the California Dream," op-ed in *San Francisco Chronicle*, July 14, 2009, p. A11.

19. "Gov. Calls for New Spending on Prisons," *Los Angeles Times*, June 27, 2006, pp. A1, A7.

20. "Rising Debt a Threat to State General Fund," *San Francisco Chronicle*, November 24, 2009, p. C3.

21. "California Bond Rating Now Lowest of Any State," *Los Angeles Times*, February 4, 2009, pp. A1, A11

LEARN MORE ON THE WEB

California Budget Project:
www.cbp.org

California state budget—Department of Finance:
www.dof.ca.gov

California state budget—Legislature:
www.lao.ca.gov

California Tax Reform Association:
www.caltaxreform.org

California Taxpayers' Association:
www.caltax.org

National Center for Education Statistics:
www.nces.ed.gov

National Governors Association:
www.nga.org

LEARN MORE AT THE LIBRARY

Jack Citrin and Isaac William Martin, eds. *After the Revolt: California's Proposition 13*. Berkeley, Calif.: Berkeley Public Policy Press, 2009.

John Decker. *California in the Balance: Why Budgets Matter*. Berkeley, Calif.: Berkeley Public Policy Press, 2009.

Joe Mathews and Mark Paul. *California Crack Up: How Reform Broke the Golden State and How We Can Fix It*. Berkeley: University of California Press, 2010.

Alvin Rabushka and Pauline Ryan. *The Tax Revolt*. Stanford, Calif.: Hoover Institution Press, 1982.

Peter Schrag. *California: America's High-Stakes Experiment*. Berkeley: University of California Press, 2006.

9

California's Local Governments: Politics at the Grassroots

CHAPTER CONTENTS

Counties and Cities

Counties

Cities

Power in the City: Council Members, Managers, and Mayors

Elections

Executive Power

More Governments

School Districts and Special Districts

Regional Governments

Direct Democracy in Local Politics

Land Use: Coping with Growth

Taxing and Spending

Local Government

The public and the media tend to focus on state and national politics, but the activities of local governments often have a greater impact on our daily lives. Our city governments make decisions about traffic on our streets; safety in our neighborhoods; and access to parks, libraries, and affordable housing. Our county governments manage transit systems and provide important social services to those most in need, including people who are homeless, mentally ill, and impoverished. Our school districts make decisions about what sorts of teachers are in our classrooms and what our children are taught.

Yet local governments are created by the state, which assigns them their rights and duties, mandating some functions and activities and prohibiting others. The state also allocates taxing powers and shares revenues with local governments. But the state can change the rights and powers granted to local governments, expanding or reducing their tasks, funding, and independence. Cities and counties are infuriated when the state tells them to do things they don't think they can afford or takes away previously committed funds to balance the state budget. School districts depend on the state for funding but are exasperated by burdensome state rules, regulations, and testing requirements.

But local government is also where we—the residents of California—have the greatest influence over our lives, simply because we are closer to it than to Sacramento or Washington, D.C. We can participate directly in local politics precisely because it's local. We can volunteer for candidates, whom we can actually meet and get to know—or we can run for office ourselves. We can lobby elected officials without relying on paid professionals. We can attend city council meetings and testify in person. We can find allies and form interest groups like those described in Chapter 4 (and all those types exist in communities). Local government is the most democratic of all levels of government, and thousands of people participate constantly—go to your own city hall and see for yourself.

COUNTIES AND CITIES

California's 58 counties and 481 cities were created in slightly different ways and perform distinctly different tasks.

Counties

California is divided into counties (see the map inside the front cover) ranging in size from San Francisco's 49 square miles to San Bernardino County's 20,164, and ranging in population from Alpine County's 1,201 residents to Los Angeles County's 10,393,185. **Counties** function both as local governments and as administrative units of the state. As local governments, counties provide police and fire protection, maintain roads, and perform other services for rural and unincorporated areas (those that are not part of any city). They also run jails, operate transit systems, protect health and sanitation, and keep records on property, marriages, and deaths. As agencies of the state, counties oversee elections, operate the courts, administer the state's welfare system, and collect some taxes.

State law prescribes the organization of county government. A county's central governing body is a five-member **board of supervisors**, whom voters elect by districts to staggered four-year terms. The board sets county policies and oversees the budget, usually hiring a chief administrator, or **county executive**, to carry out its programs. Besides the members of the board of supervisors, voters elect the sheriff, district attorney, tax assessor, and other department heads (see Figure 9.1). Conflicts often occur as the elected board tries to manage the budget and the elected executives attempt to deliver services. Unlike most of their state counterparts, these local officials are chosen in nonpartisan elections, a Progressive legacy that keeps party labels off the ballot; all serve four-year terms. As of 2010, California's 296 elected county supervisors were overwhelmingly white

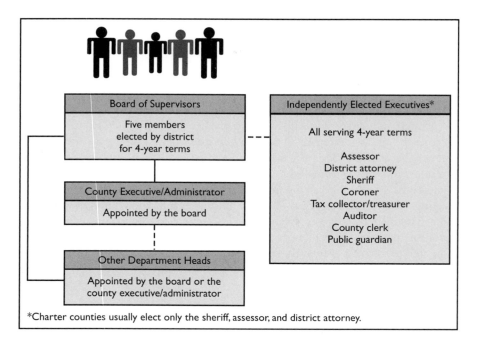

FIGURE 9.1   County Government: An Organizational Chart for California's Forty-five General-Law Counties

and male; only 23.5 percent were female, 9.5 percent were Latino, 3.4 percent were Asian, and 1.7 percent were African American. These numbers were roughly the same as in 2002, despite the growth in numbers and political engagement of some of these constituencies.

Although most counties operate under this general-law system, fourteen have used a state-provided option to organize their own governmental structures through documents called **charters**. Most of these charter counties, including Los Angeles, Sacramento, San Diego, and Santa Clara, are highly urbanized. County voters must approve the charter and any proposed amendments. Generally, a "home rule" or **charter county** uses its local option to replace elected executives with appointees of the board of supervisors or to strengthen the powers of the appointed county executive.

San Francisco is unique among California's local governments because it operates as both a city and a county. Most counties have several cities within their boundaries, but the separate city and county governments of San Francisco were consolidated in 1911. San Francisco thus has a board of supervisors with eleven members rather than a city council, but unlike any other county, it has a mayor.

No new county has been formed in California since 1907, although in some large counties such as Los Angeles, San Bernardino, and Santa Barbara, rural areas frustrated by urban domination have tried unsuccessfully to break away and form their own jurisdictions. One city in massive San Bernardino County is so far away from the city where county government is headquartered that some residents say they want to "move" to nearby Arizona.

Cities

Whereas counties are created by the state, **cities** are established at the request of their citizens through the process of **incorporation**. Starting with just 8 cities in 1850, California has 481 today. As unincorporated areas urbanize, residents begin to demand more services than their county government can provide. These may include police and fire protection, street maintenance, water, or other services. Residents may also wish to form a city to preserve the identity of their community or to avoid being annexed by some other city. Wealthy areas sometimes incorporate to protect their tax resources or their ethnic homogeneity from the impact of an adjacent big city and its economic and racial problems. California's newest city, incorporated in 2010 with a population of 47,635, is Eastvale, in Riverside County.

The process of incorporation starts with a petition from citizens who live in the area. Then the county's **local agency formation commission (LAFCO)** determines whether the area has a sufficient tax base to support city services and makes sense as an independent entity. If LAFCO approves, the county's board of supervisors holds a hearing, and then the voters of the proposed city approve or reject the incorporation.

Once formed, cities can grow by annexing unincorporated (county) territory. Sometimes, small cities that can't provide adequate services disband themselves by consolidating with an adjacent city. More rarely, residents of an existing city seek to de-annex, or secede. This was the case in the San Fernando Valley, a 222-square-mile section of Los Angeles that contains one-third of the city's population. Residents who felt isolated and ignored agitated to secede from the City of Los Angeles; their proposal was voted on in November 2002, along with a similar proposal for secession by Hollywood. Secession required approval by the voters of both these areas and the city as a whole, however, and while the San Fernando Valley narrowly supported secession, the voters of Los Angeles and Hollywood rejected the plan.

Like California counties, most California cities operate under the state's general law, which prescribes their governmental structure. **General-law cities** typically have a five-member **city council**, with members elected in nonpartisan elections for four-year terms. The council appoints a **city manager** to supervise daily operations; the manager, in turn, appoints department heads such as the police and fire chiefs (see Figure 9.2).

Cities with populations exceeding 3,500 may choose to write their own charters. A hundred and eighteen California cities have done so. A **charter city** has more discretion in choosing the structure of its government than a general-law city does, as well as somewhat greater fiscal flexibility and the freedom to set policies, provided that no state law supersedes them. All of California's largest cities have their own charters to enable them to deal with their complex problems.

Whether operating under general law or a home-rule charter, once incorporated a city takes on extensive responsibilities for local services, including police and fire protection, sewage treatment, garbage disposal, parks and recreational services, streets and traffic management, library operation, and land-use planning. The county, however, still provides courts, jails, social services, elections, tax collection, public health, and public transit.

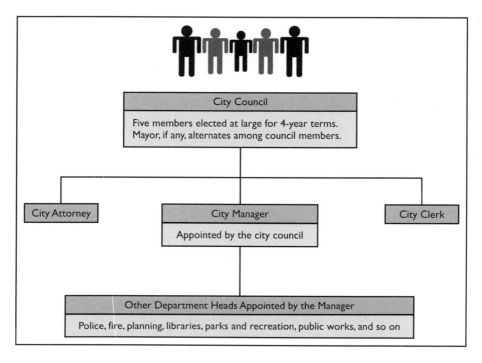

FIGURE 9.2   City Government: An Organizational Chart for California's 363 General-Law Cities

POWER IN THE CITY: COUNCIL MEMBERS, MANAGERS, AND MAYORS

Most of California's cities have five-member city councils with appointed city managers as executives, as set forth by state law. Some cities, particularly older and larger communities, have developed municipal government structures uniquely suited to their own needs and preferences. City councils, for example, may be chosen in a variety of ways or expanded in size to allow for more representation. Los Angeles has fifteen council members, San Jose ten, and San Diego eight. San Francisco's board of supervisors has eleven members. The executive office also varies among these cities; some opt for a stronger mayor rather than the manager prescribed by the state for general-law cities.

Elections

In most California cities, each council member is chosen by the whole city in **at-large elections**. This system was created by the Progressives to replace **district elections**, in which each council member represents only part of the city. At-large elections were intended to reduce the parochial influence of machine-organized ethnic neighborhoods on the city as a whole. The strategy worked, but as a result, ethnic minority candidates, unable to secure enough votes from the city as a whole to win at large, were rarely elected.

As cities grew, citywide campaigns also became extremely costly. The Progressives added to the difficulties of minority candidates and further raised the costs of campaigns by making local elections nonpartisan. This weakened the old party machines, but voters lost the modest cue provided by the listing of parties on the ballot. Furthermore, minority candidates were denied the legitimization of a party label, and campaigns cost more because candidates had to get their messages out without help from a party organization.

To increase minority representation and cut campaign costs, some cities have returned to district elections. Los Angeles has used district elections since 1924; Sacramento converted in 1971, followed by San Jose, Oakland, and later, San Diego and San Francisco. Thirty-eight California cities use some form of district elections. Most are large cities, and most have reverted to district elections through voter-approved charter amendments.

District elections increased opportunities for minority candidates in some cities, but minorities remain substantially underrepresented among California's local elected officials. Women have done somewhat better but are also underrepresented. Women and minority candidates, as well as gay and lesbian candidates, have been more successful in local elections than in state elections; they are still held back, however, by discrimination, low participation, at-large elections, high campaign costs, and the lack of party support that results from nonpartisan elections.

In most California cities, especially smaller cities that elect their councils at large, candidates who get the most votes win election even if they don't get a majority. In larger cities and cities that elect their council members by district, if no candidate wins a majority in the primary election, the top two compete in a **runoff election**, ensuring that the winner is elected with a majority of the votes. Critics object to the high cost of such elections—both to taxpayers and in campaign spending. In 2004 San Francisco responded to such criticism with **instant runoff voting**, in which voters rank candidates in order of preference. If no candidate wins a majority, the candidate with the fewest votes is eliminated and those votes are assigned to the voters' second choice—and so on until one candidate attains a majority. Oakland, Berkeley, and San Leandro—all in Northern California—have followed San Francisco's example in hopes of saving time and money and simplifying the task of voting. Other cities and counties are now considering adoption of instant runoff voting. Advocates hope that such simplification will enhance voter participation in local elections, which varies considerably from city to city. Turnout is generally higher in cities with elected mayors and district elections, but the key factor related to turnout is when the elections are held.

About one-third of California's cities hold their elections separate from state and national elections. Median turnout in these elections is less than 30 percent.[1] Los Angeles, for example, holds its elections separately, and turnout in that city's 2009 city council and mayoral contests was 18 percent. Lower turnout significantly affects outcomes because the composition of the electorate changes along with the number of voters; older, more affluent voters predominate, which usually gives an advantage to more conservative candidates. Research tells us that in cities with low voter turnout, municipal government spends less money on programs that might aid the poor. Instead, such governments fund downtown development and other projects that aid business. In short, local governments spend their revenues on those who vote.[2]

Turnout in cities that hold their elections concurrently with state and national elections is nearly twice as high.[3] The Silicon Valley city of Santa Clara started holding local elections at the same time as state and national elections in 1988, and voter turnout went from 23–24 percent to 74 percent. Unlike cities, all of California's counties hold their elections at the same time as the state and national elections. Voting for local officials may still be lower, however, due to "drop-off," with some participating voters declining to cast ballots in local races because of lack of interest or information.

As with state-level campaigns, local reformers have been concerned about the costs of city and county races and the influence of money on politics. Spending on local campaigns has risen steadily since the 1980s, when professional campaign consultants and their techniques (see Chapter 3) became common in local races. One hundred and fifty-seven California cities and counties have enacted local campaign-finance laws that require disclosure of contributors and expenditures and sometimes limit the amount of contributions. In most of these cities, the data are available to the public online. Los Angeles also restricts spending and provides limited public financing for campaigns. Long Beach, Sacramento, Oakland, Richmond, and San Francisco are also experimenting with public financing of campaigns.[4] Even in these communities, candidates and interest groups manage to raise and spend substantial sums on campaigns, often through independent expenditures or special campaign committees.[5]

Executive Power

Most people assume that mayors lead cities and have substantial power, but that's not usually the case in California communities. Because mayors were once connected with political machines, the Progressive reformers stripped away their powers, shifting executive authority to council-appointed city managers who were intended to be neutral, professional administrators. Most California cities use this **council–manager system**. While the manager administers the city's programs, appoints department heads, and proposes the budget, the council members alternate as mayor—a ceremonial post that involves chairing meetings and cutting ribbons.

San Francisco, however, uses a strong-mayor form of government, in which the mayor is elected directly by the people to a four-year term and holds powers similar to those of the president in the national system, including the veto, budget control, and appointment of department heads. San Francisco mayor Gavin Newsom exercised his powers to gain a national reputation as a leader on such issues as same-sex marriage and health insurance for all city residents—and as a platform for his successful candidacy for lieutenant governor in 2010. Los Angeles also has an empowered mayor after voters approved a new charter in 1999 giving the mayor enhanced authority, including the power to appoint forty-four department heads. Mayor Antonio Villaraigosa, elected in 2005 and reelected in 2009, thus exercises more authority than any of his predecessors. Fresno (in 1997), Oakland (in 1998), and San Diego (in 2005) have also switched to a strong–mayor form of government. Sacramento mayor Kevin Johnson has pushed for such a change in his city, but he has failed thus far to persuade the city council to put a charter amendment to the voters.

Many California cities have moved away from the pure council–manager system of government, however. While retaining their city managers, 149 California cities have revised the system so that the mayor is directly elected and serves a four-year term. Some have also increased the powers of their mayors, although they continue to sit as council members. Even without much authority, being a directly elected mayor brings visibility and influence. Mayors of San Jose, for example, exercise substantial clout despite their limited official power.

California mayors will probably continue to grow stronger, partly because of media attention but also due to the need for leadership in the tempest of city politics. Elected officials and community groups often complain about the lack of direct accountability inherent in the city manager form, in which the executive is somewhat insulated from the voters. Giving more authority to mayors and council members makes accountability more direct, but it may also decrease the professionalism of local government.

MORE GOVERNMENTS

In addition to cities and counties, California has thousands of other, less visible local governments (see Table 9.1). Created by the state or by citizens, they provide designated services and have taxing powers, mostly collecting their revenues as small portions of the property taxes paid by homeowners and businesses or by charging for their services. Yet except for school districts, most of us are unaware of their existence.

T A B L E 9.1 California's Local Governments, 2010

Type	Number
Counties	58
Cities	481
School districts	1,043
Special districts	4,776
TOTAL	6,358

SOURCE: California State Controller, www.sco.ca.gov, and Ed-Data, www.ed-data.ca.us.

School Districts and Special Districts

In California, 1,043 local governments called **school districts** provide education. They are created and overseen by the state and governed by elected boards, which appoint professional educators as superintendents to oversee day-to-day operations. Except for parents and teachers, whose involvement is intense, voter participation in school elections and politics is low. One challenge for the schools is that while the majority of students are Latino, Asian, or African American, a majority of those who vote in school elections and the majority of school board members are non-Hispanic whites.[6]

Of the $66.7 billion in school spending in 2009–2010, the state supplied 58 percent, the federal government provided 14 percent, and 28 percent came from local property taxes and other local sources.[7] Just two years earlier, local governments provided only 21 percent of school funding, providing a poignant example of where the state's budget crisis has left these governments with more responsibilities. The shift has not been without costs. In 2010, 16 percent of the state's school districts were declared "at risk" because of inadequate funding, and California has ranked low among the states in per-pupil spending for years.[8] These figures refer to funds for salaries and operating expenses. Money for building repairs and construction of new schools comes mostly from **bonds** (borrowed money paid by local taxes), which until recently required approval by a two-thirds majority of the voters. Following the Proposition 13 tax revolt, such approvals became rare; in 2000, however, voters approved lowering the percentage required for approval to 55 percent, and passing bonds became easier.

Special districts are an even more common form of local government, with no fewer than 4,776 in California. Unlike cities and counties, which are "general-purpose" governments, special districts usually provide a single service. California law provides for fifty-three different types of special districts, ranging from water and waste disposal districts to hospital and cemetery districts. They are created when citizens or governments want a particular function performed but either have no appropriate government agency to perform the service or choose not to delegate it to a city or county. Sometimes special districts are formed when small communities share responsibilities for fire protection, sewage treatment, or other services that can be more efficiently provided on a larger scale. Depending on the nature of the special district, funding usually comes from property taxes or charges for the service that it provides. The number of special districts increased when Proposition 13 imposed tax constraints on general-purpose local governments, because some services can be funded more easily in this way. Their impacts in terms of taxes and services have been considerable. Altogether, California's special districts spend $39.6 billion a year, while California's cities spend $57 billion and its counties spend $48.4 billion.

A city council or a county board of supervisors governs some special districts, but most are overseen by a commission or board of directors that may be elected or appointed by other officials. Like a school board, this body usually appoints a professional administrator to manage its business. Accountability to the voters and taxpayers is a problem, however, because most of us aren't even aware of these officials.

Regional Governments

The existence of so many sorts of local governments means that many operate in every urban region of California. The vast urban areas between Los Angeles and San Diego or San Francisco and San Jose, for example, consist of many cities, counties, and special districts, with no single authority in charge of the whole area. Los Angeles County alone hosts eighty-eight cities and two hundred special districts. This fragmentation creates small-scale governments that are accessible to citizens, but that are sometimes too small to provide services efficiently. In addition, problems such as transportation and air pollution go far beyond the boundaries of any one entity.

Many California cities deal with this situation by **contracting for services** from counties, larger cities, or private businesses. Cities in Los Angeles County, for example, may pay the county to provide any of fifty-eight services, from dog catching to tree planting. Small cities commonly contract with the county sheriff for police protection rather than fund their own forces. Contracting allows such communities to provide needed services while retaining local control, although some see the system as unfair because wealthy communities can afford more than poor ones.

Another solution to urban fragmentation is **consolidation**, or the merger of existing governmental entities. With voter approval, small school districts, special districts, or even cities can unite to provide services more efficiently. In the past consolidation has occurred mostly with school districts, but proposals for consolidations have become more common lately due to California's prolonged budget crisis.[9]

Special districts are yet another way to address fragmentation and regional problems—particularly problems, such as air pollution and transportation, that extend beyond the boundaries of existing cities or counties. For example, California has forty-seven transit districts that run bus and rail systems. Most are countywide, but some, including the Bay Area Rapid Transit (BART) system, cover several counties.

Twenty of California's urban areas also have **councils of government (COGs)**, in which all of the cities and counties in the region are represented. The biggest COGs are the six-county Southern California Association of Governments (SCAG) and the nine-county Association of Bay Area Governments (ABAG) in Northern California. These regional bodies focus on land-use planning and development. Because they can't force their plans on cities and counties, though, they serve mainly as forums for communication and coordination among the jurisdictions they encompass.

As regional problems have grown and competition among cities has increased, the need for regional planning has also grown. The state has asserted its authority over local governments to require the implementation of regional plans through agencies such as ABAG and SCAG. Other state-created agencies, such as the Metropolitan Water District and the South Coast Air Quality Management Board in Southern California, exercise great power. Reformers sometimes advocate the creation of multipurpose regional governments, perhaps by merging existing regional special districts, to provide government capable of dealing with area-wide issues including transportation, air quality, and growth; however, existing cities firmly oppose any loss of local control.

DIRECT DEMOCRACY IN LOCAL POLITICS

Direct democracy is used even more locally than statewide. Between 1995 and 2008 an average of 428 local ballot measures were voted on by Californians each year.[10] All charter changes—such as increasing the powers of the mayor or introducing district council elections—are subject to voter approval. Voters must also approve proposals for local governments to introduce or raise taxes or to borrow money by issuing bonds. Charter changes require a simple majority, but a supermajority of two-thirds is required for most taxes. Resulting from a series of statewide initiatives, these requirements have severely restricted the ability of local governments to raise money, because voter approval on funding issues is difficult to win.

Most local measures are placed on the ballot by a city council, county board of supervisors, or school board. They include tax measures and charter amendments, but the most common measures have to do with education (usually seeking additional funding). Citizens also put proposals to the voters through the initiative process, although initiatives constitute only a tiny percentage of local measures. Most often, the initiatives are attempts to control growth or amend charters. Some are frivolous, like the 2008 San Francisco initiative that proposed renaming the city sanitation facility the "George W. Bush Sewage Plant," but most are more serious. District elections, for example, were introduced in some cities by initiative, as were **term limits** (usually restricting elected officials to two 4-year terms). Several California counties and over forty cities now limit the terms of elected officials. As a last resort, voters may express their dissatisfaction with elected officials through recall elections. Recalls of local officials are rare, however, averaging fewer than a dozen a year, even after the dramatic recall of the governor in 2003.[11]

Land Use: Coping with Growth

One of the most frequent uses of direct democracy in California cities and counties is by citizens seeking to control growth. Deciding how land can be used is a major power assigned to local governments by the state. The way they use this power affects us all. If local governments encourage growth in the form of housing, industry, or shopping centers, for example, the economy may boom, but streets may become clogged, schools overcrowded, sewage treatment plants strained, and police and fire protection stretched too thin. When this happens, environmentalists or residents who merely expect adequate services may grow frustrated and demand controls on growth. If the city council or county board of supervisors is unresponsive, discontented groups may take their case to the voters through an initiative.

Since 1971, when development became a major local issue, almost all California communities have enacted some form of growth control. The battle typically pits a grassroots coalition with little money against big-spending developers and builders. The recent recession brought growth to a halt in most communities, decreasing the salience of this issue, but even so the cities of Buellton, Pleasanton, and San Juan Capistrano approved growth limits and protections for open space in 2008.

TAXING AND SPENDING

The way local governments raise and spend money reveals a great deal, not only about what they do but also about the limits they face in doing it.

The biggest single source of money for California's local governments was once the **property tax**, an annual assessment based on the value of land and buildings. Then, in 1978, taxpayers revolted with **Proposition 13**, a statewide initiative that cut property tax revenues by 57 percent. Cities adjusted by cutting jobs and services to save money. Many introduced or increased **charges for services** such as sewage treatment, trash collection, building permits, and the use of recreational facilities. Such charges are now the largest source of income for most cities (see Figure 9.3), followed by the sales tax, which returns 2 percent of the state's basic 8.25 percent sales tax to the city or county where the sale occurs. Some counties add to the base sales tax to fund transportation. Some cities and counties have also added taxes on hotel rooms, utilities, or other things. In 2009 voters in Oakland approved a tax on the sale of medical marijuana, undoubtedly setting a precedent for other cities.

The shift from property taxes to other sources of revenue also affects local land-use decisions. When a new development is proposed, most cities now prefer retail businesses to housing or industry because of the sales taxes that such businesses generate. This trend has been labeled the **fiscalization of land use** because instead of choosing the best use for the land, cities opt for the one that produces the most revenue.

With more legal constraints on their taxing powers, counties had an even rougher time after Proposition 13. State aid to counties increased slightly, but with no alternative local taxes readily available after the passage of Proposition 13, most counties cut spending deeply. Years later, they are still struggling to provide essential services. Like cities, most counties increased charges and fees for services.

Over half of county revenues come from the state and federal governments (32.5 percent and 19.4 percent, respectively), but this money must be spent on required programs such as social services, health care, and the courts. Even so, state and federal aid does not cover the cost of these mandatory services, leaving counties with little money to spend as they choose.

Just as the revenue sources of cities and counties differ, so do their spending patterns, largely because the state assigns them different responsibilities. As you can see in Figure 9.3, public safety is the biggest expenditure for California cities, whereas welfare is the biggest county expenditure.

Although Proposition 13 is much loved by homeowners for reducing property tax bills, the initiative caused serious fiscal problems for local governments by cutting property tax revenues and making approval of new taxes or tax increases more difficult. That combination necessitated severe budget cuts for cities and counties. Beyond that, Proposition 13 gave the state the responsibility to

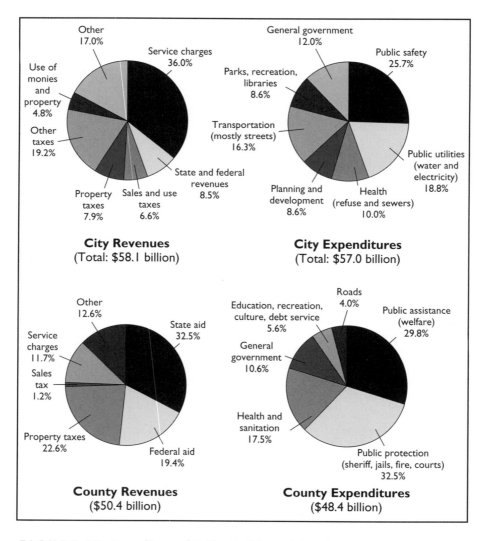

FIGURE 9.3 Expenditures of California Cities and Counties, 2007–2008

SOURCE: California State Controller, 2010, www.sco.ca.gov.

allocate property taxes among local governments even as Proposition 98 (see Chapter 8) mandated allocation of a fixed percentage of the state budget to education. As a consequence, a portion of property taxes that had previously gone to cities and counties was shifted to schools—putting even further pressure on city and county budgets and resulting in further cuts in services. Moreover, cities and counties, which previously had some control of their own revenues, became dependent on the state for property and sales tax revenues, a significant loss of local control.[12]

These problems were compounded when successive recessions hit California in the early 1990s and again in 2001–2003 and 2009–2010. Facing massive deficits, the state balanced its budget by "take-backs" of local property tax revenues totaling billions of dollars. In 2004 Governor Arnold Schwarzenegger exacerbated circumstances for local governments by reducing vehicle license fees, which had previously been a significant source of local revenues.

Cities were so frustrated by all this that they pushed for a way to lock in their revenues through a constitutional amendment to guarantee future revenues and prevent such state take-backs. Voters approved **Proposition 1A** in 2004. Local governments hoped it would give them greater financial security in the future, but in the 2009 fiscal crisis, the state diverted nearly $4 billion in local property taxes from schools, cities, counties, and redevelopment agencies. Under Proposition 1A the state must eventually repay these funds, but in the short term the action only worsened the fiscal problems of local governments. Cities and counties responded in 2010 with **Proposition 22** banning state borrowing from local governments and won voter approval.

Meanwhile, California cities and counties have been pushed to the fiscal brink. Vallejo (near San Francisco) declared bankruptcy in 2008 when tax revenues dropped and the city couldn't meet its commitments to employee salaries and benefits. In 2010 Oakland laid off over 10 percent of its police force, despite its high crime rate. Facing a $529 million deficit, Los Angeles mayor Antonio Villaraigoso, usually an ally of public employees, proposed layoffs and demanded salary concessions from the city's unions. Maywood, in Southern California, laid off all its city employees, including police officers, and contracted with other cities for some services and with Los Angeles County for police protection. "We will become 100 percent a contracted city," said Maywood's interim city manager.[13] Other cities also considered contracting for services. Redding, in Northern California, and Santa Clarita, in Southern California, for example, contracted with a private company to provide library services. Still other cities considered merging police or fire departments with neighboring cities. In some areas, reformers called for consolidation of small school districts, special districts, and cities as a partial solution to budget problems.

Cities from San Diego to San Jose, along with many other local agencies, also faced fiscal strain due to the pensions and other benefits they had offered their employees when their budgets were flush with cash. Now unable to meet these commitments but bound by contracts, local governments, like the state (see Chapter 8), are seeking to renegotiate the contracts to win concessions from current employees or to move to a two-tier pension system, preserving benefits for current workers but reducing them for future hires.

Despite their fiscal trials, local governments remain a major component of the California economy, with nearly 1.3 million employees (half are in education)[14] and combined budgets totaling over $212 billion. Local governments cost a lot, but they also do a lot.

LOCAL GOVERNMENT

The state limits what local governments can do, as demonstrated by Proposition 13 and ongoing budget battles. Some may dispute such interventions, but the state's authority remains supreme. At the same time, local governments can lead the way to innovations in public policy, as illustrated by San Francisco's health insurance policy, Long Beach's public financing for campaigns, and Oakland's tax on medical marijuana. California's political system gives residents many opportunities to decide what sort of communities they want, and many Californians take advantage of these opportunities by engaging in local politics.

NOTES

1. Zoltan L. Hajnal, Paul G. Lewis, and Hugh Louch, "Municipal Elections in California: Turnout, Timing, and Competition," Public Policy Institute of California, March 2002, www.ppic.org.

2. Jessica Trounstine and Zoltan Hajnal, "Low Voter Turnout Does Matter: Spending Priorities in Local Politics" (paper presented at the annual meeting of the Midwest Political Science Association, Chicago, April 2004).

3. Hajnal, Lewis, and Louch, *op. cit.*

4. Jessica Levinson, "Local Public Financing Charts" (Los Angeles: Center for Governmental Studies, May 2009), www.cgs.org (accessed July 13, 2010).

5. See Center for Governmental Studies, *Money and Power in the City of Angels,* July 2010, www.cgs.org (accessed July 16, 2010).

6. Belinda I. Reyes, "Demographic Change and the Politics of Education in California," in *Racial and Ethnic Politics in California*, ed. Sandra Bass and Bruce M. Cain (Berkeley: Berkeley Public Policy Press, Institute of Governmental Studies, University of California, 2008), pp. 236, 241.

7. EdSource, www.edsource.org (accessed July 14, 2010).

8. California Department of Education, www.cde.ca.gov (accessed July 14, 2010). For California's rank among the states on education spending, see Public Policy Institute of California, *California 2025*, www.ppic.org (accessed July 14, 2010), or California Budget Project, "School Finance Facts," June 2010, www.cbp.org (accessed July 14, 2010).

9.   For more on regional fragmentation and special districts, see Brian, P. Janiskee, "The Problem of Local Government in California," in *California Republic*, ed. Brian P. Janiskee and Ken Masugi (Lanham, Md.: Rowman and Littlefield, 2004).

10. California Elections Data Archive, Institute for Social Research, California State University, Sacramento, www.csus.edu/isr (accessed July 15, 2010).

11. *Ibid.*

12. For further discussion of these effects of Proposition 13, see John Decker, *California in the Balance* (Berkeley, Calif.: Berkeley Public Policy Press, 2009), pp. xi, 116, 137–138.

13. "Maywood to Lay Off All City Employees, Dismantle Police Department," June 22, 2010, www.latimesblogs.latimes.com/lanow/2010/06.

14. U.S. Census, www.census.gov/govs/apes (accessed July 16, 2010).

LEARN MORE ON THE WEB

ABZY News Links (listing state and local media and online news sources):
www.abyznewslinks.com/uniteca.htm

California Elections Data Archive (CEDA) (information on local elections):
www.csus.edu/isr/reports/california_elections/index.html

California State Association of Counties:
www.csac.counties.org

California State Controller (data on cities, counties, schools, and special districts):
www.sco.ca.gov

Councils of Government (COGs):
Association of Bay Area Governments (ABAG):
www.abag.org

Southern California Association of Governments (SCAG):
www.scag.ca.gov

On instant runoff voting (IRV):
www.instantrunoff.com

League of California Cities:
www.cacities.org

Public Policy Institute of California (studies on local government):
www.ppic.org

LEARN MORE AT THE LIBRARY

Terry Christensen and Tom Hogen-Esch. *Local Politics: A Practical Guide to Governing at the Grassroots*. Armonk, N.Y.: M. E. Sharpe, 2006.

Jack Citrin and Isaac William Martin, eds. *After the Tax Revolt: California's Proposition 13 Turns 30*. Berkeley, Calif.: Institute of Government Studies, 2009.

Paul G. Lewis. *Deep Roots: Local Government Structure in California*. San Francisco: Public Policy Institute of California, 1998.

Paul Lewis and Max Neiman. *Cities under Pressure: Local Growth Controls and Residential Development Policy*. Public Policy Institute of California, www.ppic.org, 2002.

10

State-Federal Relations: Conflict, Cooperation, and Chaos

CHAPTER CONTENTS

California's Clout with the President

California's Clout with Congress

   Divisiveness

   Controversy over the Proposed Auburn Dam—Case in Point

Terrorism

Immigration

Climate Change

Water

Shared Resources

California Today: Golden State or Fool's Gold?

California's uniqueness stems in part from its position as the nation's most populated state; it also emanates from the state's vast resources, size, diversity, and engagement in thorny issues. We see problems and their outcomes on a scale here that is unequaled elsewhere. And so it is with the state's relationship with the federal government, which can be described as wary, uneven, and often fraught with controversy.

Sometimes state and national leaders differ about how California should be managed. Public education reform is one such controversial policy area, with the federal government and state legislature at odds over the definition of *reform*. On other issues, such as water policy, however, officials from the two governments have worked well together. There are also instances where California has moved forward with its own response to national issues, with the federal government eventually moving into line; nowhere is this more obvious than with environmental protection. Deciding the best responses to problems that affect both the nation and state can be a challenge because, like its forty-nine counterparts, California is both a self-governing entity and a member of the larger national government.

Matters become even more complicated when attempts are made to determine financial responsibility for costly issues such as massive transportation projects, immigration control, or homeland security, to name a few. Because the state is so large and complex, federal assistance almost always seems inadequate. When federal aid or programs are cut, California seems to suffer disproportionately compared with other states.

Nevertheless, when the state confronts a complex issue, its internal battle is often the harbinger of similar concerns likely to affect the rest of the nation. The women's right-to-choose movement, gun control, political reform, the tax revolt, medical marijuana, stem cell research, and same-sex marriage all had early beginnings—and in some cases, origins—in California.

In this chapter we review California's impact on national policymaking and policy actors. We also explore some of the critical policy areas that test California's relationship with the federal government: immigration, greenhouse gas emissions, and the distribution of federal resources to the state of California. Each topic touches on the delicate balance between state autonomy and national objectives—perspectives in federalism that are not always viewed the same ways by state and federal government leaders. These issues are important not only because of their present urgency but also because of their effects on California's Clout with the President, Obama visited California on eleven occasions.

CALIFORNIA'S CLOUT WITH THE PRESIDENT

Despite its size and huge bloc of Electoral College votes, California hasn't figured prominently in presidential elections in recent years, largely because the state has been predictably secure for Democratic candidates in every election since 1992. As a consequence, we don't see as much of the candidates in California as voters do in other states. Republican presidential candidates do not invest significant resources on California because they don't see much return, and Democrats stay away because of their need to pursue electoral votes in more competitive states. But California is important to both national political parties in one major respect—namely, as the top state for campaign contributions. That alone keeps candidates coming, albeit infrequently, to places such as Orange County, Silicon Valley, and Hollywood.

California has had an uneven relationship with the nation's presidents. Democrat Bill Clinton, who benefitted from California's then fifty-four electoral votes in 1992 and 1996, funneled discretionary federal funds to California, particularly in the areas of high-tech research and defense industry projects. Clinton was also pro-choice, pro–gun control, and environmentally sensitive—themes that resonate with most Californians. None of this was lost on the California electorate, which supported Democratic candidates Al Gore in 2000 and John Kerry in 2004 over the winner, Republican George W. Bush.

Republican president George W. Bush approached California with a different point of view than Clinton, largely due to his general hands-off attitude on domestic policy issues. For example, the Bush administration rejected California's claim of illegal electricity price hikes in 2001, although the courts eventually found otherwise. Other areas of disinterest on the president's part included agriculture, border patrol assistance, and terrorism funding. Even the election of fellow Republican Arnold Schwarzenegger in 2003 failed to bond the two Republican leaders except in the most cosmetic fashion. Given the clash of cultural and political values between most Californians and the conservative Republican president, it's easy to see why the distance between the state and the president was more than a matter of miles. Bush visited California fewer than two dozen times during his presidency, compared with seventy visits by Clinton in his eight years in office.

The administration of Democrat Barack Obama falls somewhere between Clinton's "love fest" for and Bush's seeming indifference to California. On the one hand, Obama has been sensitive to the role of technology in California and called for extension of the soon-to-expire $74 billion research and development tax credit immediately upon assuming office. The Obama administration has also embraced California's strict rules on automobile exhaust emissions, a move completely opposite to the approach of George W. Bush. On the other hand, the Obama administration has been willing to compensate California for only a fraction of the hundreds of millions of dollars spent on the incarceration of illegal immigrants awaiting transport to their home countries. And California was unsuccessful in wresting any of the $4.35 billion in Obama's "Race to the Top" education improvement funds at a time when public education has been gasping for support. During the first two years of his administration, Obama visited California on eleven occasions.

CALIFORNIA'S CLOUT WITH CONGRESS

As the nation's most populated state, California has fifty-three members in the House of Representatives, dwarfing the delegations of every other state. Texas and New York are second and third, with thirty-two and twenty-nine members, respectively. The majority party in each house of Congress chooses committee chairs who, in turn, control the flow of national legislation. Republicans possessed a majority of seats between 1995 and 2007, resulting in the accumulation of considerable power. By 2005 Californians held a record six chairmanships of the twenty-one standing committees. Then the political winds shifted.

In 2006 growing discontent with the war in Iraq, an uneven national economy, and political corruption in Congress led the nation's voters to elect a

Democratic majority to the House of Representatives. San Francisco's Nancy Pelosi, elected in 2002 to the post of minority leader of the House, was chosen to be Speaker. With that election, she assumed the highest national leadership ever held in the United States by a woman. As a result of the election outcome, several prominent California Democrats assumed key committee chairmanships by virtue of their years of seniority in the House.

Political party fortunes took a turn in 2010 when the Republicans captured control of the House and increased their minority in the Senate. As of 2011, Republicans were poised to gain at least three chairmanships: Oversight and Governmental Reform (Darrell Issa); Armed Services (Howard "Buck" McKeon; and Appropriations (Jerry Lewis). In addition, Kevin McCarthy was elected majority whip, the third highest party post after speaker and majority leader.

The political winds also have shifted in the U.S. Senate, but not as much as in the House. Although the upper house is a bit less partisan than the lower house, the majority party still controls all committee chairmanships, and therefore the flow of legislation. In 2006 the off-year revolution produced a slim 51-to-49 Democratic majority, thanks to the cooperation of two independents who promised their loyalty to the Democratic side of the aisle. Suddenly, Senators Dianne Feinstein and Barbara Boxer, both first elected in 1992, emerged as key players on issues dealing with the environment, foreign relations, and the judiciary. By 2009 the Democratic majority hit 60, a number larger enough to cut off filibusters. Within a year, however, the supermajority was lost with the death of Massachusetts senator Ted Kennedy.

Democrats in California enjoy a comfortable margin of 34–19 over Republicans in the House of Representatives. In other respects California's congressional makeup is as diverse as the rest of the state. As of 2011, the delegation includes seven Latinos, four African Americans, and three Asians; nineteen women are members of the delegation. Both of California's U.S. senators are women as well.

The Republican ascendancy to power in the House opens the way for a new chapter in governance at the national level. With divided government, Republicans and Democrats find themselves with tough choices: either cooperate on major issues in the name of consensus or hold out with gridlock as the outcome. Consideration of each strategy is important, given the upcoming national election in 2012.

Divisiveness

One other fact must be added to the discussion of Californians in Washington: historically, the state's **congressional delegation** has been notoriously fractured in its responses to key public policy issues affecting California. Much of the conflict stems from the makeup of the districts. North/south, urban/suburban/rural, and coastal/valley/mountain divisions separate the state geographically. Other differences exist, too, in terms of wealth, ethnicity, and basic liberal/conservative distinctions. To be sure, no congressional district is completely homogeneous, yet most members of Congress tend to protect their districts' interests more than those of the state as a whole. Thus, on issues ranging from desert protection to immigration, California's representatives have often canceled each other's votes, leaving states such as Texas far more powerful because of their relatively unified stances. Even on foreign trade, members from California often have worked at cross-purposes, depending on the industries, interest groups, and demographic characteristics of their districts.

Only on the question of offshore oil drilling have most members of the state's delegation voted the same way. In 2008, with gasoline prices hitting record levels, President Bush called for an end to the twenty-seven–year federal moratorium on offshore drilling. Almost the entire California delegation opposed the proposal, and the damaging Gulf of Mexico offshore oil blowout in 2010 silenced any further discussion.

Controversy over the Proposed Auburn Dam—Case in Point

The struggle over the proposed Auburn Dam in Northern California is a current case in point. California hungers for more water, but the real debate has been over the best ways to get it and at what cost. The massive $9.6 billion proposal has been considered in Congress since 1960. Federal agencies have spent $325 million just on feasibility studies. Yet California lawmakers in Washington have remained paralyzed over the issue, due in no small part to the conflicting objectives of environmentalists and farmers. The various sides struck a compromise in 2003 by upgrading another dam downstream. But concerns over California's weakened levee system led House Republican Dan Lungren to pursue the idea yet again in 2007 after the release of a 152-page report by the U.S. Department of the Interior.[1] Meanwhile, Democrats Pete Stark and George Miller have used their clout with the majority to thwart consideration of the project as an environmentally unsound proposal. The issue of whether the project is a boondoggle or a vital flood-control program is not as significant as the fact that it has polarized the California congressional delegation. As a result, while Californians have fussed among themselves over this vexing question, representatives from other states have worked in bipartisan ways to garner federal dollars for their projects.

TERRORISM

September 11, 2001, represented a turning point in American history. Never before had terrorists penetrated onto American soil in such a punishing way. As expected, the federal government took the lead in responding to this unprecedented event. With passage of the USA Patriot Act on October 26, 2001, the national government assumed expanded powers to search out terrorism and terrorist-related activities in the areas of hazardous substances, money laundering, illegal immigration, cyber crime, fraud, and other areas. Acting under these new powers, the U.S. attorney general asked states and local governments to help in detaining and questioning suspicious persons; the new Transportation Security Administration assumed security responsibilities at the nation's airports; and the U.S. Border Patrol increased its vigilance against illegal entry. Statewide, between 2002 and 2010, the Governor's Office of Homeland Security distributed more than $1.3 billion in federal funds for state and local equipment and training.

Although the federal government has picked up much of the tab, the states have been burdened with significant costs, too, and are likely to see those costs continue well into the future. From transportation systems and port security to water pipelines and canals to electricity lines, California's infrastructure now requires additional protection against terrorists. As a result, the state has absorbed major security obligations without federal funding. For example, the Real ID Act, a federal law requiring states to issue universal driver's licenses, has an estimated price tag in California of $500 million to $750 million between 2008 and 2013, yet only a small fraction of the cost was funded by the federal government.[2] Such costs are difficult for governments to swallow in good economic times, and with California plagued by out-of-balance budgets for most of the time between 2002 and 2011, they have made a major dent in available resources.

The state's surge in congressional chairmanships has somewhat helped California's position with the federal government on homeland security allocations. Following the September 11 terrorist attacks on the United States, the federal government made antiterrorism funds available to all fifty states. With $5.03 per capita for the 2004–2005 fiscal year, California ranked last despite its coastal location, huge seaports, nuclear power plants, massive power line grids, and other targets that are ripe for terrorist attacks. Meanwhile, Wyoming ranked first with $37.94 per capita, followed by Vermont ($31.56 per capita), North Dakota ($30.81 per capita), and Alaska ($30.42 per capita). Hard work by Senator Feinstein and California House Republican leaders produced a new method of allocation at the Department of Homeland Security. Thus, for the 2006–2007 fiscal year, California climbed to twenty-first place, with $6.81 per capita. Meanwhile, Vermont took over first place, with $20.03 per capita; Wyoming dropped to second, with $18.06.[3] Since then, the Obama administration has promised to review the funding formula in recognition of high-risk states such as California, but serious economic issues have prevented the development of new legislation.

IMMIGRATION

California has long been a magnet for those in search of opportunity. And they have come—first the Spanish; then Yankee, Irish, and Chinese immigrants during the nineteenth century; followed by Japanese, Eastern European, African American, and Vietnamese immigrants beginning in the 1970s, Asian Indians in

T A B L E 10.1 California's Immigrants: Leading Countries of Origin, 2006

Country	Number
Mexico	4,396,000
Philippines	750,000
China	659,000
Vietnam	446,000
El Salvador	396,000
Korea	323,000
India	303,000
Guatemala	241,000
Iran	182,000
Taiwan	163,000
Canada	134,000
United Kingdom	126,000

SOURCE: U.S. Decennial Census, 2005.

the 1990s, and more Latinos throughout the last half century (see Table 10.1). But over the past two decades, several independent events have converged to influence the moods of the state's residents and would-be residents. Lack of opportunity in other nations has led millions to choose California as an alternative; meanwhile, an overburdened and underfunded infrastructure has led many of those already here to oppose further immigration. Much of the antipathy has been directed at Latinos—particularly those from Mexico—but anger has also been aimed at Asians.

The numbers are substantial. Whereas 15.1 percent of California's population were foreign born in 1980, 27 percent fell within that category in 2010, with projections showing that percentage remaining in place through 2030.[4] During the same period, the percentage of foreign-born residents of the United States as a whole edged up from 6.2 to 12.1 percent (see Figure 10.1). Between 1990 and 2005 California's population grew by between 500,000 and 600,000 annually, and more than 40 percent of that number came from foreign immigration. In 2010 the Pew Hispanic Center estimated that there were between 11.4 million and 12.4 million illegal immigrants nationwide, with between 2.5 million and 2.85 million of them in California.[5] Between 1990 and 2008 the percentage of illegal immigrants living in California dropped from 42 percent to 22 percent, indicating greater movement to other states.[6]

With these dramatic events reshaping California, experts have argued about whether the immigrants help or harm the state's economy. For example, one recent study finds that only about one-third of recent immigrants have health

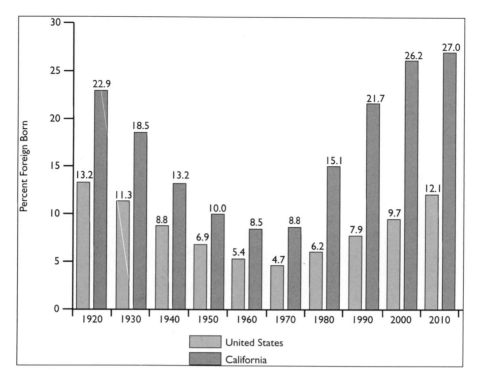

FIGURE 10.1 Population of Foreign-Born Residents, California and United States Comparison

insurance, suggesting a financial burden for public health institutions and services.[7] At the same time, other studies show that immigrants—legal and illegal combined—are very similar in economic makeup to the rest of America.[8] Moreover, in some industries, such as California farming, illegal immigrants are critical to harvests, making up as much as 90 percent of the workforce. To the extent that these workers are prevented from laboring in the fields, California's $36 billion agriculture industry could suffer irreparable damage.[9] All these findings suggest a growing ambivalence toward the illegal immigration issue in California.

None of this has stopped the federal government from moving on immigration, although observers disagree about the appropriate level of federal involvement. In 2008 the Bush administration increased surveillance of U.S. companies with illegal immigrant employees, leading to fines for employers, imprisonment for undocumented workers, and workforce shortages in some industries.[10] At the same time, between a more vigilant border protection system and a declining U.S. economy, the number of attempted border crossings by illegal immigrants declined.[11]

The largest issue related to immigration is determining which level of government should assume responsibility for its costs. While the federal government has long established the criteria for immigration and the conditions for enforcement, it leaves the states responsible for meeting the needs of immigrants. Nowhere does this contradiction ring louder than in California. Among unauthorized immigrants alone, recent estimates cite health-care costs of $1 billion, education costs for 400,000 of their children at $1 billion, and incarceration costs for 18,000 illegal immigrants at $500 million.[12] Few of these costs have been picked up by the federal government, yet their day-to-day impact is a reality.

Controversy continues over how much responsibility California should assume for stemming the tide of illegal immigration. In 2006 President Bush asked Governor Schwarzenegger to send 2,500 members of the National Guard to Arizona and New Mexico to help U.S. Border Patrol agents. The governor dispatched only 1,000 troops, arguing that the rest were needed at home to assist in cases of wildfires, earthquakes, or other unanticipated calamities.[13] Clearly, the role of each government in managing the immigration question remains a tough issue to sort out.

CLIMATE CHANGE

California and the federal government have had a rocky relationship with respect to climate change. At times, the state has fought national objectives; at others, California has taken the lead. No example of state resistance is more obvious than the issue of air quality. According to the U.S. **Environmental Protection Agency (EPA),** the ten smoggiest counties in the nation are found in California. Metropolitan Los Angeles, an area that extends east to Riverside and south to Long Beach, tops the list as the smoggiest area in the nation. Actually, the number of "unhealthful" days in the L.A. basin has declined from an average of 189.6 during the 1996–1998 period to 141.8 during the period of 2006–2008, according to the American Lung Association, although progress has stopped since 2004.[14] Statewide, the costs have been great. One recent study finds that annual losses in California from unhealthy air amount to $28 billion in the form of premature deaths, illness, and lost productivity in the workplace.[15]

Congress and the EPA have been unhappy with the inability of the state to move forward on clean air. But given the state's dependence on manufacturing, particularly in the vast Los Angeles basin, it has been difficult to meet national standards without choking off the local economy. In 1992 state regulators in Southern California established the Regional Clean Air Incentives Market Program (RECLAIM), a program in which manufacturers buy and sell emissions permits as a means of encouraging emissions reduction. The program has led to substantial reductions in environmental decay,[16] although the region remains far from healthy.

The state has enjoyed more success in the area of auto emissions, although at times the road has been bumpy for other reasons. California has a history of leading the nation in reducing auto emissions, which account for 28 percent of the state's greenhouse gases. Since the passage of the original Clean Air Act of 1970, state environmental regulators have asked for and received forty-four waivers from the EPA to establish standards beyond federal requirements. That's what happened until 2007, when the Bush administration–guided EPA ruled that there was no evidence suggesting that auto emissions contained greenhouse gases,[17] to the amazement of most scientists in the United States and worldwide. Since the agency gave no scientific explanation for its ruling, California and sixteen other states sued the EPA for not carrying out its mandate. The United States Supreme Court agreed, and thus began another chapter in the struggle for control over emissions standards.

The political environment regarding auto emissions changed dramatically with the election of Barack Obama to the presidency in 2008. Early in 2009 he asked his new EPA administrator to review previous decisions on California's waiver petitions. In June 2009 the EPA approved California's proposal and announced a new national policy on higher gasoline mileage and lower emissions by 2017, based on California's standards. On this occasion, at least, California set the trend for the rest of the nation.

WATER

Not all of California's jurisdictional disputes have occurred with the federal government. In several areas, the state has tangled with other states. The storage of nuclear waste and agriculture rules are two such examples of interstate fights, but no argument has as much significance as California's struggle for freshwater. Three-quarters of California's water comes from north of Sacramento. Three-quarters of the water is consumed south of the capital. For this transfer to work, water must move, and it does so thanks to two giant systems. The federal Central Valley Project, which dates from 1937, supplies the farmers of the southern Central Valley. The State Water Project, begun in 1960, largely supplies southern urban areas. Both systems intercept freshwater near the Sacramento–San Joaquin Delta before it can flow out to the ocean through San Francisco's Golden Gate. Given the state's huge population and pivotal role in agriculture, water is a resource that California can ill afford to do without, and that fact has led to ugly entanglements.

The linchpin of the water dispute between California and other states is the Colorado River, the freshwater source that begins in Colorado and winds through six other states. Under a 1922 multistate agreement, California is entitled to 4.4 million acre-feet, or 59 percent, of the lower basin river annually. Yet according to some critics, California exceeded its share by as much as 800,000 acre-feet per year, enough to provide for the annual water needs of 1.6 million households in rapidly growing nearby states such as Arizona and Nevada.[18]

Fearing an all-out water war that would spill into Congress, officials from seven states held talks for eighteen months to resolve the problem. In 2000 they agreed to a formula that would allow California to gradually reduce its consumption of the excess over a fifteen-year period. During the transition, officials from Arizona offered to "bank" surplus water for California, should the state require it. But with Arizona, Nevada, and other western states growing faster than any other parts of the nation, it remains to be seen how long the fragile agreement will remain in play. At least for the time being, the seven western states have solved a troublesome issue without federal participation.

Meanwhile, the federal government's Department of the Interior and the state of California worked to resolve the ongoing three-way battle among agribusiness (which uses 80 percent of the state's water consumption), environmentalists seeking to preserve rivers and deltas, and urban areas in need of water to grow. Under the auspices of CalFed, a joint federal and state water agency, the two governments developed a plan in 2000 to expand existing federal reservoirs in California, improve drinking water quality, and develop a creative water recycling program. Most of the $8.5 billion price tag will be borne by the federal government, with Californians providing $825 million from the passage of Proposition 50 in 2002. In 2004 Congress reauthorized CalFed, with a commitment of $10 billion over thirty years to improve the quality of water flowing into the Sacramento Delta and San Francisco Bay.

Uncertainties remain, however. In 2002 the U.S. Department of the Interior modified a plan previously favored by environmentalists. The new plan sent more water from the Central Valley Project to farmers, rather than using it for ecosystem restoration. Still, water can only be distributed to customers if it is available, and recent droughts in California and the West have left the region thirsty. The issue has become so important that in 2007, responding to a record-low snowpack in the Sierra Nevada Mountains and concern for the welfare of endangered species, a federal court judge reduced deliveries of Northern California water to Southern California by 25 percent. The impact of the order put Southern California governments on notice: until water supplies could be assured, major construction projects in that portion of the state would be put on hold.[19] So the battle over water continues, not only between California and the federal government but also between farmers, environmentalists, and developers.

SHARED RESOURCES

The word **federalism** refers to the multifaceted political relationship that binds the state and national governments. One aspect of that relationship centers on financial assistance that wends its way from federal coffers to state and local treasuries, and that amounted to about $653 billion in fiscal year 2010. The preponderance of this assistance comes in the form of **grants-in-aid**, amounting to about 20 percent of all state and local government revenues. This assistance is the result of more than six hundred federal programs designed to assist states in areas ranging from agricultural development to high-tech research. For decades, California received more than its fair share of grants-in-aid from the federal government. With defense- and space-related research serving as a huge economic magnet, the Golden State obtained more money from the federal government than it sent in.

That has changed. In 1983 California had 10 percent of the national population but received 22 percent of the national government's expenditures. Then came the slide: with a pared defense budget, cutbacks in infrastructure work, and the push for a balanced budget, federal contributions have shrunk considerably over the past two decades. As of 2007 California had 12.1 percent of the nation's population but received 11.8 percent of the nation's federal funds. The state now ranks thirty-seventh in the distribution of federal spending on a per capita basis—down sharply from twentieth in 1990.[20]

There is another way to appreciate the changing relationship between the federal government and California. Because of the state's massive growth and receipt of federal assistance in highway and water projects and environmental protection, California had a long history of getting more dollars from the federal government than it contributed. Beginning in 1986, however, California became a "donor" state. Ever since, California has contributed more money to the national treasury than it has received, and the disparity is increasing every year. In 1992, for every dollar California sent to Washington, D.C., the state received 93 cents in federal goods and services. In 2005, for every dollar California sent to Washington, only 78 cents came back in goods and services, leaving the state in forty-third place in per capita federal spending (see Table 10.2). No matter how you slice it, California is getting less of the federal "pie" today than in the past.

But there is more to the story than just numbers; it's the kind of numbers that make a huge difference. Data compiled in 2006 found that if the cost of living is added to the mix, more than 16 percent of all Californians fall under the poverty line, compared with about 12 percent nationwide.[21] And when we

T A B L E   10.2   Federal Expenditures per Dollar of Taxes, Fiscal Years 1992 and 2005—California and Selected States

	Expenditures per Dollar of Taxes		Ranking	
	FY1992	FY2005	FY1992	FY2005
New Mexico	$2.08	$2.03	11	1
Maryland	$1.27	$1.30	15	18
Kansas	$1.05	$1.12	27	22
Texas	$.93	$.94	37	35
Massachusetts	$1.01	$.82	31	40
California	$.93	$.78	38	43
New Jersey	$.66	$.61	50	50

SOURCE: Tax Foundation.

consider that the state's immigrant population is more than twice the national average on a per capita basis, it becomes clear that the state's needs fare particularly poorly when it comes to federal funding.

The data presented here fly in the face of the political posturing that has emerged from both Congress and the presidency in recent years. Instead, they show a California with unlimited potential, and a California that has been much better for some than others. They reveal a state that in recent years has given much more to the federal government in taxes than it has received in programs and services. They also reflect the fragmentation that has haunted the state's congressional delegation on virtually every issue except offshore oil drilling. As a result, California's "Golden State" nickname has a different meaning in Washington than in California—namely, sizable economic resources that have landed disproportionately in the federal treasury.

CALIFORNIA TODAY: GOLDEN STATE
OR FOOL'S GOLD?

Is today's California still the state with unlimited potential or the state with too many burdens to survive? When it comes to relations with the federal government, perhaps the answer is a little of both. California is king when it comes to campaign contributions for national candidates, research and development, the center of agriculture, and auto emissions standards. At the same time, California is a pauper in matters of dealing with a perpetual state budget deficit, a dilapidated infrastructure, and a frayed social safety net. Once upon a time, the state would have looked to the federal government for rescue, and the federal government would have been happy to help. That relationship has been replaced by one in which the state and federal government are often at odds, and occasionally in sync.

Some of the shift has been because of the ebb and flow of national politics. By most accounts, California is a "blue" (Democratic) state when it comes to national elections. Thus, during the Clinton years, the state benefitted from extra federal attention on research and development tax credits, H1–B visas, and even some defense contracts. During the Bush years, California didn't fare so well, as attested by the administration's disregard for the state's immigration issues, anti-terrorism concerns, and exorbitant electricity bills.

We're still sifting the relationship with Democratic president Barack Obama, although there are some early hints of an uptick in the relationship. The Obama administration has backed off on prosecuting for marijuana possession, supported continuation of the research and development tax credit, and sent hundreds of millions of federal dollars to help California homeowners deal with foreclosure issues. At the same time, California has not fared well in capturing a chunk of federal dollars in the Race to the Top education reform program. Moreover, the state did not do so well in capturing a large share of the $787 billion in economic stimulus funds provided in the American Recovery and Reinvestment Act passed in 2009. Whereas the state had the fourth highest unemployment rate, it ranked eighteenth in per capita funding.

If nothing else, California operates more independently of the federal government today than in the times of heavy government defense spending. To this extent the state has been weaned of federal dependence. The process may not have been enjoyable, but the state has become more self-reliant as a result. To that end, California's growing autonomy may be the hallmark of the state's direction in the coming years. Whatever the future, it will be an interesting experiment.

NOTES

1. U.S. Department of Interior, "Reclamation: Managing Water in the West, Auburn–Folsom South Unit Special Report," December 2006.

2. For example, for fiscal 2009 the entire federal commitment to all fifty states plus the District of Columbia was $48,575,000, of which California received a small percentage. See Department of Homeland Security, "Driver's License Security Program," www.dhs.gov/files/programs/gc_1214423542432.shtm.

3. Dowell Myers, John Pitkin, and Julie Park, *California Demographic Features* (Los Angeles: School of Policy, Planning, and Development, University of Southern California, February 2005), p. ix.

4. U.S. Census Bureau, *Statistical Abstract of the United States: 2009* (Washington, D.C.: Government Printing Office, 2008), p. 19.

5. "Report: One in 10 Workers in California Is Illegal," *Sacramento Bee*, April 15, 2010, pp. A1, A20.

6. "Illegal Immigrants Become Subject of Coverage Debate," *San Francisco Chronicle*, September 11, 2009, pp. A1, A18.

7. *The Size and Characteristics of the Unauthorized Migrant Population in the U.S.* (Washington, D.C.: Pew Hispanic Center, 2006), p. 9.

8. "Immigrants in the Work Force: Study Belies Image," *New York Times*, April 10, 2010, pp. A1, A3.

9. "Border Policy Is Pinching Farmers," *Los Angeles Times*, September 22, 2005, pp. C1, C2.

10. See "Bush Orders Some Firms to Show Workers' Status," *Wall Street Journal*, June 10, 2008, p. A6; and "Shortage of Skilled Workers Looms in U.S.," *Los Angeles Times*, April 21, 2008, p. A1, A7.

11. "Crossings by Migrants Slow as Job Picture Dims," *Wall Street Journal*, April 9, 2008, pp. A1, A12.

12. "These data are cited in Bernard L. Hyink and David H. Provost, *Politics and Government in California*, 16th ed. (New York: Pearson Longman, 2004), p. 233.

13. "Gov. Refuses Bush Request for Border Troops," *Los Angeles Times*, June 24, 2006, pp. A1, A18.

14. "Smog in L.A. Still Tops in Nation," *Los Angeles Times*, April 28, 2010, pp. AA1, AA6.

15. California Healthline, November 13, 2008, www.californiahealthline.org.

16. See Daniel A. Mazmanian, "Achieving Air Quality: The Los Angeles Experience" (unpublished paper, University of Southern California, March 2006), p. 28.

17. "E.P.A. Says 17 States Can't Set Greenhouse Gas Rules for Cars," *New York Times*, December 20, 2007, pp. A1, A30.

18. "California Water Users Miss Deadline on Pact for Sharing," *New York Times*, January 1, 2003. The six states in addition to California are Arizona, Colorado, Nevada, New Mexico, Utah, and Wyoming.

19. "Enforcing Recent Water Laws May Throttle State's Growth," *Los Angeles Times*, January 14, 2008, pp. B1, B8.

20. U.S. Census Bureau, *op. cit.,* table 467.

21. Deborah Reed, "Poverty In California," *California Counts* 7, no. 4 (May 2006), www.ppic.org.

LEARN MORE ON THE WEB

California and federal taxes:
www.taxfoundation.org

California Institute for Federal Policy Research:
www.calinst.org

Environmental Protection Agency:
www.epa.gov

Immigration:
www.irps.ucsd.edu

Office of Management and Budget:
www.whitehouse.gov/omb

U.S. House of Representatives:
www.house.gov

U.S. Senate:
www.senate.gov

LEARN MORE AT THE LIBRARY

Larry N. Gerston. *American Federalism: A Concise Introduction.* Armonk, N.Y.: M. E. Sharpe, 2007.

Robert F. Nagel. *The Implosion of American Federalism.* New York: Oxford University Press, 2001.

Laurence J. O'Toole. *American Intergovernmental Relations: Foundations,* Perspectives, *and Issues.* 4th ed. Washington, D.C.: CQ Press, 2007.

G. Ross Stephens and Nelson Wikstrom. *American Intergovernmental Relations: A Fragmented Federal Polity.* New York: Oxford University Press, 2007.

Glossary

at-large elections City council elections in which all candidates are elected by the community as a whole rather than by districts.

attorney general The top law enforcement officer and legal counsel; the second most powerful member of the executive branch.

bank and corporation tax A tax on the profits of lending institutions and businesses; the third most important source of state revenue.

bicameral legislature Organization of the state legislature into two houses: the forty-member senate (elected for four-year terms) and the eighty-member assembly (elected for two-year terms).

Big Five The governor, assembly speaker, assembly minority leader, senate president pro tem, and senate minority leader, who gather together informally to thrash out decisions on the annual budget and other major policy issues.

Board of Equalization The five-member state board that maintains uniform property tax assessments and oversees the collection of sales, gasoline, and liquor taxes; members are elected by district; part of the executive branch.

board of supervisors The five-member governing body of counties; elected by district to four-year terms.

bonds Subject to voter approval, state and local governments can borrow money by issuing bonds, which are repaid (with interest) from the general fund budget or from special taxes or fees.

bureaucracy State or local government workers employed through the civil service system rather than appointed by the governor or other elected officials.

central committees Political party organizations at county and state levels; weakly linked to one another.

charges for services Local government fees for services such as sewage treatment, trash collection, building permits, and the use of recreational facilities; a major source of income for cities and counties since the passage of Proposition 13 in 1978.

charter city or county A local government that drafts its own structures and organization through a document like a local constitution (also known as a "home-rule" charter), subject to voter approval.

charter The equivalent of a constitution for a local government; includes government structures, election systems, powers of officeholders, conditions for employing local government workers, and often much more.

cities Local governments in urban areas, run by city councils and mayors or city managers; principal responsibilities include police and fire protection, land-use planning, street maintenance and construction, sanitation, libraries, and parks.

Citizens Redistricting Commission Enacted by the voters in Proposition 11 (2009), this commission will assume responsibility for determining the boundaries of state legislative districts and Board of Equalization districts.

city council The governing body of a city; members are elected at large or by district to four-year terms.

city manager The top administrative officer in most California cities; appointed by the city council.

civil service system A system for hiring and retaining public employees on the basis of their qualifications or merit; replaced the political machine's patronage, or spoils, system; encompasses 98 percent of state workers.

closed primary An election of party nominees in which only registered party members may participate.

collegiality Deferential behavior among justices as a way of building consensus on issues before the court.

Commission on Judicial Appointments A commission to review and make recommendations on the governor's nominees for appellate and supreme courts; consists of the attorney general, the chief justice of the state supreme court, and the senior presiding judge of the courts of appeal.

Commission on Judicial Performance The state board empowered to investigate charges of judicial misconduct or incompetence.

conference committee A committee of senate and assembly members that meets to reconcile different versions of the same bill.

congressional delegation Members of the House of Representatives and Senate representing a particular state.

consolidation The merger of cities, school districts, or special districts; usually requires voter approval.

Constitution of 1849 California's first constitution, which was copied from constitutions of other states and featured a two-house legislature, a supreme court, and an executive branch including a governor, lieutenant governor, controller, attorney general, and superintendent of public instruction, as well as a bill of rights. Only white males were allowed to vote.

Constitution of 1879 California's second constitution, which retained the basic structures of the Constitution of 1849 but added institutions to regulate railroads and public utilities and to ensure fair tax assessments. Chinese individuals were denied the right to vote, own land, or work for the government.

constitutional amendments May be placed on the ballot by a two-thirds vote of the legislature or through the initiative process; must be approved by a simple majority of the voters.

constitutional convention An occasion for extensive revision or reform of the state constitution. A two-thirds vote of the state legislature is required to put a proposal for a convention on the ballot. If voters approve, delegates are elected by district.

contract lobbyist An individual or company that represents the interests of clients before the legislature and other policymaking entities.

contracting for services Smaller cities contract with counties, special districts, other cities, or private companies to provide services they cannot efficiently provide themselves.

controller An independently elected state executive who oversees taxing and spending.

council–manager system A form of government in which an elected council appoints a professional manager to administer daily operations; used by most California cities.

councils of government (COGs) Regional planning organizations with representation for cities and counties.

counties Local governments and administrative agencies of the state, run by elected boards of supervisors; principal responsibilities include welfare, jails, courts, roads, and elections.

county executive The top administrative officer in most California counties; appointed by the board of supervisors.

courts of appeal Three-justice panels that hear appeals from lower courts.

cross–filing An election system that allowed candidates to win the nomination of more than one political party; eliminated in 1959.

demographic groups Interest groups based on race, ethnicity, gender, or age; usually concerned with overcoming discrimination.

direct democracy Progressive reforms giving citizens the power to make and repeal laws (initiative and referendum) and to remove elected officials from office (recall).

direct mail A campaign technique by which candidates communicate selected messages to selected voters by mail.

director of finance The state officer primarily responsible for preparation of the budget; appointed by the governor.

district attorney The chief prosecuting officer elected in each county; represents the people against the accused in criminal cases.

district elections Elections in which candidates are chosen by only one part of the city, county, or state.

economic groups Interest groups with sizable financial stakes in the political process who seek to influence legislators and other public policymakers.

Environmental Protection Agency (EPA) The federal government body charged with carrying out national environmental policy objectives.

executive order The power of the governor to make rules that have the effect of laws; may be overturned by the legislature.

Fair Political Practices Commission (FPPC) Established by the Political Reform Act of 1974, this independent regulatory commission monitors candidates' campaign finance reports and lobbyists.

federalism The distribution of power, resources, and responsibilities among the national, state, and local governments.

fiscalization of land use Cities and counties, when making land-use decisions, opt for the alternative that produces the most revenue.

general elections Statewide elections held on the first Tuesday after the first Monday of November in even-numbered years. Voter turnout is higher than in primary elections and highest during presidential elections.

general-law city or county A city or county whose organization and structure of government are derived from state law.

general veto The gubernatorial power to reject an entire bill or budget; overruled only by an absolute two-thirds vote of both houses of the state legislature.

ghost voting When legislators cast electronic votes in place of assembly members who are not at their posts; this practice is against the law.

governor California's highest-ranking executive officeholder; elected every four years.

grants-in-aid Payments from the national government to states to assist in fulfilling public policy objectives.

gut-and-amend The process of removing the original provisions from a bill and inserting new, unrelated content.

"hourglass economy" The tendency of the California economy to include many people doing very well at the top, many barely getting by at the bottom, and fewer and fewer in the middle; symptomatic of California's vanishing middle class.

incorporation The process by which residents of an urbanized area form a city.

independent expenditures Campaign spending by interest groups and political action committees on behalf of candidates.

initiative A Progressive device by which people may put laws and constitutional amendments on the ballot after securing the required number of voters' signatures.

instant runoff voting Voters rank candidates in order of preference. If no candidate wins a majority, the candidate with the fewest votes is eliminated, and those votes are assigned to the voters' second choice—and so on until one candidate attains a majority.

insurance commissioner An elected state executive who regulates the insurance industry; created by a 1988 initiative.

interest group An organized group of individuals sharing common political objectives who actively attempt to influence policymakers.

item veto The power of the governor to delete or reduce the budget within a bill without rejecting the entire bill or budget; an absolute two-thirds vote of both houses of the state legislature is required to override.

judicial activism Making policy through court decisions rather than through the legislative or electoral process.

Judicial Council Chaired by the chief justice of the state supreme court and composed of twenty-one judges and attorneys; makes the rules for court procedures, collects data on the courts' operations and workload, and gives seminars for judges.

legislative analyst An assistant to the legislature who studies the annual budget and proposed programs.

legislative committees Small groups of senators or assembly members who consider and make legislation in specialized areas such as agriculture or education.

legislative counsel Assists the legislature in preparing bills and assessing their impact on existing legislation.

legislative initiatives Propositions placed on the ballot by the legislature rather than by citizen petition.

lieutenant governor The chief executive when the governor is absent from the state or disabled; succeeds the governor in case of death or other departure from office; casts a tiebreaking vote in the senate; is independently elected.

litigation An interest group tactic of challenging a law or policy in the courts to have it overruled, modified, or delayed.

lobbying Interest group efforts to influence political decision makers, often through paid professionals (lobbyists).

local agency formation commission (LAFCO) A county agency set up to oversee the creation and expansion of cities.

logrolling A give-and-take process in which legislators trade support for each other's bills.

mayor The ceremonial leader of a city; usually a position that alternates among council members, but in some large cities the mayor is directly elected and given substantial powers.

nonpartisan elections A Progressive reform that removed party labels from ballots for local and judicial offices.

open primary Voters may cast their ballots for any listed candidate for an office irrespective of the voters' party affiliation; the top two vote winners proceed to a runoff in the general election; instituted by a 2010 ballot measure to take effect in 2012.

personal income tax A graduated tax on individual earnings adopted in 1935; the largest source of state revenues.

plea bargaining An agreement between the prosecution and the accused in which the latter pleads guilty to a reduced charge and lesser penalty.

political action committees (PACs) Mechanisms by which interest groups direct campaign contributions to preferred candidates.

political consultants Expert professionals in political campaigning available for hire; most consultants work exclusively for candidates of one of the major political parties.

Political Reform Act of 1974 An initiative requiring officials to disclose conflicts of interest, campaign contributions, and spending; also requires lobbyists to register with the Fair Political Practices Commission.

preprimary endorsement Political parties' designation of preferred candidates in party primary elections, thus strengthening the role of party organizations in selecting candidates; banned by state law until 1990.

president pro tem The legislative leader of the state senate; chairs the Rules Committee; selected by the majority party.

primary elections Elections to choose nominees for public office; held in June of even-numbered years. Voter turnout is typically low.

Progressives Members of an antimachine reform movement that reshaped the state's political institutions between 1907 and the 1920s.

property tax A tax on land and buildings; until the passage of Proposition 13 in 1978, the primary source of revenues for local governments.

Proposition 1A (2004) A ballot measure designed to prevent the state from taking revenues from local governments in times of fiscal stress.

Proposition 8 (2008) An initiative that amended the state constitution to restrict marriage to opposite-sex couples.

Proposition 11, the Voters FIRST Initiative (2008) An initiative that placed legislative redistricting in the hands of a fourteen-member citizens commission instead of the state legislature.

Proposition 13 (1978) Also known as the Jarvis-Gann initiative; a ballot measure that cut property taxes and significantly reduced revenues for local governments.

Proposition 22, the California Defense of Marriage Act (2000) A ballot initiative that declared marriage an act between a man and a woman.

Proposition 22, the Local Taxpayers, Public Safety and Transportation Act (2010) An initiative that keeps the state government from taking local government funds.

Proposition 34 (2000) A legislative initiative setting contribution limits for individuals and political action committees; commonly circumvented through independent expenditures.

Proposition 58 (2004) A proposition that set broad spending limits on state government and required the state to gradually set aside up to 3 percent of all revenues in a "rainy day" fund.

Proposition 98 (1988) An initiative awarding public education a fixed percentage of the state budget.

Proposition 140 (1990) An initiative limiting assembly members to three 2-year terms and senators and statewide elected officials to two 4-year terms and cutting the legislature's budget.

Proposition 187 (1994) An initiative reducing government benefits for illegal immigrants; parts of Proposition 187 were declared unconstitutional by federal courts in 1995.

Proposition 209 (1996) An initiative that eliminated affirmative action in California.

Proposition 227 (1998) An initiative limiting bilingual education to no more than one year.

public defender A county officer representing defendants who cannot afford an attorney; appointed by the county board of supervisors.

public interest groups Organizations that purport to represent the general good rather than private interests.

reapportionment The adjustment of legislative district boundaries to keep all districts equal in population; done every ten years after the national census; done by a citizens commission beginning in 2011.

recall A Progressive reform allowing voters to remove elected officials by petition and majority vote.

redistricting Another term for *reapportionment*, the adjustment of legislative districts by population every ten years.

referendum A Progressive reform requiring the legislature to place certain measures before the voters, who may also repeal legislation by petitioning for a referendum.

register to vote Citizens who are over eighteen years of age and who are not incarcerated or in a mental institution are eligible to sign up to vote by completion of a registration form. Nearly 30 percent of those eligible to register in California do not do so and thus cannot participate in elections.

Reynolds v. Sims A 1964 United States Supreme Court decision that ordered redistricting of the upper houses of all state legislatures by population instead of land area.

Rules Committee See *Senate Rules Committee*.

runoff election When no candidate receives more than 50 percent of the vote in a nonpartisan primary for trial court judge or local office, the top two candidates face each other in a runoff.

sales tax A statewide tax on most goods and products; adopted in 1933; local governments receive a portion of this tax.

school districts Local governments created by states to provide elementary and secondary education; governed by elected school boards.

secretary of state An elected state executive who keeps election records and supervises elections.

Senate Rules Committee A five-member committee consisting of the senate president pro tem and two other members from each party in the senate; assigns chairs and committee appointments; functions as the gatekeeper of most senate legislation.

Silicon Valley The top area for high-tech industries; located between San Jose and San Francisco.

single-issue groups Organized groups with narrow policy objectives; not oriented toward compromise.

Southern Pacific Railroad A railroad company founded in 1861; developed a political machine that dominated California state politics through the turn of the century.

speaker of the assembly The legislative leader of the assembly; selected by the majority party; controls committee appointments and the legislative process.

special districts Local government agencies providing a single service, such as fire protection or sewage disposal.

special session A legislative session called by the governor; limited to discussion of topics specified by the governor.

state auditor An assistant to the legislature who analyzes ongoing programs.

superintendent of public instruction The elected state executive in charge of public education.

superior courts Lower courts in which criminal and civil cases are first tried.

supreme court California's highest judicial body; hears appeals from lower courts.

term limits Limits on the number of terms that officeholders may serve; elected executive branch officers and state senators are limited to two 4-year terms, and assembly members are limited to three 2-year terms. Some local elected officials are limited to two or three 4-year terms.

termed out An elected official must leave office when he or she has completed all the terms of office allowed under California's term limits law.

third parties Minor political parties that capture a small percentages of the vote in the general election but are viewed as important protest vehicles.

"three strikes" A 1994 law and initiative requiring sentences of twenty-five years to life for anyone convicted of three felonies.

treasurer The elected state executive responsible for managing state funds between collection and spending.

user taxes Taxes on select commodities or services "used" by those who benefit directly from them; examples include gasoline taxes and cigarette taxes.

veto See *general veto* and *item veto*.

vote by mail Voters who prefer not to vote at their polling places or who are unable to vote on Election Day may apply to their county registrar of voters for an absentee ballot and vote by mail; nearly half of those who vote in California elections vote by mail.

voter turnout The proportion of eligible and/or registered voters who actually participate in an election. When turnout is high, the electorate is usually more diverse and liberal; when it is low, the electorate is usually older, more affluent, and more conservative.

Workingmen's Party Denis Kearney's antirailroad, anti-Chinese organization; instrumental in rewriting California's constitution in 1879.

Index